Christian, Non-Fiction
62,847 Words

Copyright 2013, Joseph Smetana

ISBN# 978-1-6192767-7-2

Joseph Ministries
Rockwall, TX 75087
www.josephministries.org

This page intentionally blank

Table of Contents

Introduction

As I look at what I've written covering the last twenty years of my life, I am amazed at what God has done. The life that I live today is so different and so much better than where I started. I would not trade what I have today for anything. It is the pearl of great worth (see Matthew 13:44-46). I am living in my promised land.

This promised land I speak of is for everyone who is willing to seek first God's kingdom and His righteousness. It is not just for a select few. It is not just for preachers. It is for you, if you are willing to make the journey.

It may help to understand the make-up of this book before you begin reading. The first two chapters are introductory and provide background on my personal journey and how God started me and directed me on this path. Chapter 3 provides the biblical foundation for the kingdom of God on earth. Chapters 4 through 11 go into details on the covenant names of God, who God is according to who He says He is and give examples from my personal life of how I came to know Him, not just about Him, in a real way relative to each of His names. Chapter 12 puts this all together providing you the path and direction of what it takes to enter your own promised land. Chapter 13 provides a practical method of how to apply this in your life and start your own journey. The final chapter expounds upon the blessings of the Lord in the kingdom of God and then gives us a scriptural warning.

What I've written here represents everyday life. In my case, the message I bring of the promised land is from the perspective of an engineer working in corporate America. Yes, God can even work in an engineer's life! He can also work in your life. No matter what you do, you also can go into your promised land.

The testimonies that I've included here are just a small sampling of what God has done. God has done and continues to do much in my life. My hope is that the message I bring will enable you to have your own similar testimonies just a few years from now. Come with me now as I share the path to the promised land, the kingdom of God.

Chapter 1
A Cry for Help

I have surely seen the affliction of my people which are in Egypt, and have heard their cry (Exodus 3:7)

The year was 1984, and the day turned out to be a different kind of day for me. Normally, I was not a praying man. I had grown up in a very religious Catholic family. When I was younger, there was some generally unspoken pressure to at least consider becoming a Catholic priest. I went to a Catholic elementary school. Two of my Aunts were Catholic nuns. At one point in my mother's life, she had even committed to become a nun. Obviously, that didn't happen, as I am here today and have 3 sisters. Prayer, as I was taught it, was saying "Our Fathers" or "Hail Mary's", possibly praying the rosary or similar scripted prayers. It had never done much for me, and I pretty much abandoned this type of praying in my teenage years. When I thought about God, or spoke to Him, it was usually an "Oh God help!" type of prayer. To be honest, I'm not sure I ever really expected an answer. Looking back, I realize that I actually had some answers that I didn't recognize to be God. In the Catholic Church, the message, at least to me, was that Jesus died for my sins and because of His sacrifice, I would go to heaven when I died. The unspoken message that came across essentially was "Do your best to be good, work hard, and when you die you'll go to heaven. Don't really expect God to intervene in your life." This is how I lived. It was also the way I saw the people around me live. This probably was not intended, but this was the message I received.

But today was a different kind of day for me. I had just gone through the toughest two years of my

3

life. About two years earlier, my wife had left, apparently with some other man, taking my two young sons with her. I came home from work the day after a payday to find the bank accounts cleaned out, anything of value gone, including most of the bedroom furniture (which she had just convinced me to sell a day or two earlier), a jar full of change, worth maybe $50.00 and a "Dear John" letter. I was in shock! My emotions were a wreck! In many ways, it seemed my life was destroyed. I was deeply hurt and angry. I was also in financial trouble. The bills due immediately were at least ten times the amount of money I had. It turned out that she had gone to Florida, and here I was, a US Navy officer, stationed in Bremerton, Washington, about as far away as one could get and still be in the country.

And I was a faithful family man. My upbringing had put a strong sense in me that divorce was wrong and I should try to restore my marriage. As it turned out, I probably should have gone to court, sued for divorce based on abandonment, and ended the whole thing. But I didn't believe in that. I wanted my family back. Of course, I had no idea how to do this. For a while, I didn't even know where she went. The only thing that kept me from totally losing it was my job. It consumed me. As a nuclear engineer in the Navy doing a shipyard overhaul, it was easy to be consumed by the job. There was so much work to do. I didn't want time off. Home was misery and loneliness, just awful. I also missed my two little boys. I'd rather work and keep my mind focused on something else.

Finally, about 6 months had passed, and I received a message on the ship from my wife. "I love you. Please call me" it said. Hope rose up. I made the call, and she told me "I want to come home. I need money for the trip." I didn't have any money to send, so I went to Navy Relief and borrowed the amount needed and sent it. When she finally showed up in town a few weeks later, I was expecting her to come home. Instead, she stayed somewhere else. After about 2 days she came by, dropped off my boys, and left. I was glad to see them, but this was not what I had in mind. It wasn't what she had in mind either. A few days later I was subpoenaed to appear in court for a legal separation hearing. I had no idea what I was in for! The court kicked me out of my house and required me to pay maintenance and child support amounting to about 80% of my after tax salary! After paying my monthly car payment, there was less than $20 left over! I moved onto the ship, which, with the overhaul nearing completion, was barely fit to live on. It was often quite noisy from the work going on around. I learned to sleep with earplugs in. I ate on the ship, and my food bill to the officer's mess got to be months behind. Fortunately, my time in service ultimately resulted in a raise and promotion from Ensign to Lieutenant Junior Grade allowing me to begin to catch up. All the while I attempted to restore my marriage. This set me up once again.

As the overhaul completed, the ship was set to move home port to San Diego. My wife told me she wanted to go with me and things were greatly improved. For a few days, we acted like a family again. I set up with the Navy to move the household goods to San Diego and went with the ship there. My wife was to follow with the kids in a few weeks after taking care of the move. She met me in San Diego, but with a huge surprise. She was not coming. She had redirected the movers to move the household goods to another house in Washington State only a few miles from Bremerton. I exploded, but it was no use.

After about 10 months in San Diego and out at sea, I completed my qualification as a Surface Warfare Officer and requested a transfer to the USS Bainbridge that was going into overhaul in Bremerton. This was an easy sell for the Navy. Officers don't generally volunteer for shipyard duty, particularly if they'd already been through an overhaul. All this time, I was legally separated, but not divorced from my wife. I was going to give one more attempt at restoring my marriage. It didn't take long for it to be clear this was not going to work. She showed up at the appointment I made with a marriage counselor only to categorically state it was over, she was going to get a divorce, and that was that. She could have told me that up front and saved me the $75 fee for the counselor.

Well, it didn't end there. On one night a month or two later, while I was picking up my sons for the weekend, I noticed on the counter a *completed* and court approved divorce along with a marriage license for what had become her live in boyfriend. I lost it! I hadn't agreed to any of this. In fact, I had been attempting to save money to fight for custody of my boys. How could this be? It was time to find a lawyer, a *good* lawyer. I found a good Jewish lawyer rather quickly. The first thing he did was tell me that a custody battle for my children was going to cost me a lot and he needed a thousand dollar deposit before he would even begin, to make sure I was serious. He also warned me that the Washington State laws were very much against me and the odds were not in my favor. Once he took me as a client, it took about one week to have the divorce thrown out of court. Then we started the custody battle. I managed to get joint custody during the custody battle, where I had my sons for two weeks out of every four. When they were with me, I lived in a furnished mobile home. When they were not, I lived in the bachelor officer's quarters. This took quite a number of months. Eventually, I lost the custody battle.

So here I was, cleaning up the mobile home to turn back over to the owner, since I no longer needed it as my sons would no longer be staying with me for extended time periods. As I cleaned it, the reality of what had happened sunk in. I had lost everything that mattered. My dreams were shattered. I would not be able to raise my sons. I could not handle it any more. I found myself on my knees crying out to God for all I was worth. I don't know how long I prayed. I do know it was quite a while, might have been an hour, might have been four. I don't remember much of what I said to God. But I remember pouring my heart out to Him and pleading for help. One thing I remember is a desperate cry for "something real", referring primary to a real love, a worthwhile life.

After this time in prayer, something changed. I was able to go on. I really didn't know where to or what for, but I could go on. I was able to look to a new life, a new future. I didn't know what that meant. I had already submitted my resignation from the Navy, and that was effective in a few more months. I went out and purchased a Yamaha DX7 synthesizer and started focusing more on my music. Little did I know how much my steps were being ordered of the Lord. This was a turning point in my life. I didn't know it, but I was on my way to the promised land, the kingdom of God. I want to share this journey with you. I want you to come too. I promise you it will be better than anything you have ever imagined.

Again, the kingdom of heaven is like unto treasure hid in a field; the which when a man hath found, he hideth, and for joy thereof goeth and selleth all that he hath, and buyeth that field. Again, the kingdom of heaven is like unto a merchant man, seeking goodly pearls: Who, when he had found one pearl of great price, went and sold all that he had, and bought it.
(Matthew 13: 44-46)

Chapter 2
The Lord Directs My Path

*A man's heart deviseth his way: but the LORD
directeth his steps. (Proverbs 16:9)*

Normally, a minimum of six months notice is required to resign from being an officer in the Navy. I had given them a little more notice than that, and after the child custody battle was over, most of that time still remained. I decided that not only did I not want to be in the Navy anymore, but, after looking at the state of the nuclear power industry, and knowing the demands of that industry, I decided I would also get out of the nuclear power business. This was a big decision. It meant that instead of approximately doubling my salary in roughly a year that I would take a pretty significant pay cut. Looking at the industry options I decided that I wanted to work in the high tech electronics industry.

I linked up with a headhunter (a professional career placement service) that specialized in finding jobs for junior military officers planning to leave the military. After writing my resume, I attended a career fair in San Francisco where I interviewed with a number of companies including Avantek, Raychem, and Texas Instruments. All of these companies expressed an interest in me. I really didn't want to move to Texas, so I focused on pursuing the opportunities with Avantek and Raychem, both of which were located in the Silicon Valley area of California.

Initially, Avantek was the most aggressive. They actively interviewed me for two different positions. I was quickly offered a manufacturing supervisor job at Avantek in an area that primarily tuned microwave circuits. After reviewing the job, I told them I wasn't interested, that the position would not be challenging enough for me. When I did that, they stopped interviewing me for the other position that I was much more interested in. I reviewed this with the headhunter and he told me that they considered this as me not wanting to work for Avantek.

Raychem was very active. I interviewed with them at least 3 separate times (maybe more, it's been a long time since then), which is amazing considering that I was living in Washington State and they had to fly me to California to interview. The last time that I was there, we talked about salary, whom I would work for, where my office would be, etc. I was promised that a written offer would be in the mail in a few days. I was ready to take it. It seemed exactly like the kind of job I wanted. A week passed and the offer had not come. Another week and I called my headhunter. He said he'd call and find out. The next day, he called and told me what was going on. His message was that they very much wanted to hire me, but the day after my last interview the company started a hiring freeze. They weren't allowed to hire me. I didn't know it at the time, but this is a pretty common thing for major corporations to do at the end of the year.

So now it was December, and I was leaving the Navy at the end of January and didn't have a job. It was time to see if Texas Instruments was still interested. They flew me down for an interview and described to me a rather challenging opportunity that got my interest, in spite of being in Dallas. I was pretty sure they would offer me the job, but I had concerns. Texas Instruments was known as "tiny income" by many. The headhunter told me that a good offer from them would be $28,000 per year based on his experience placing other junior military officers with them. I hadn't even discussed salary with them. This was much less than the other companies I had interviewed with. After estimating the living costs in Dallas and my various needs, I decided that if they offered me at least $30,500 per year, I would take it. Even that would be almost a 40% cut in take home pay. When the offer came, it was exactly $30,500 per year. You would think that they were looking over my shoulder when I did my calculations. I can tell you today who *was* looking over my shoulder.

I moved to Texas in February and started working for Texas Instruments. For some reason, I seemed to know just where I wanted to live and had no trouble finding a suitable apartment in Garland about ten miles from my office. The job was good and things were going okay. I thought about going to church a number of times, but never did. When I was in Washington, I went to different churches occasionally, but never really got hooked up with one. If someone asked me, I'd go. If not, I usually didn't go. At one point, I even pulled out the phone book and looked at the various Christian church listings, but I knew so little about the various denominations. So now I was in Texas. I remember telling God one day that I had no idea how to find a good church. If He wanted me in church, He would just have to show me where.

A couple of months had passed, and virtually the only people I knew were people I worked with. When I was off work, I was often lonely. I had a few men friends, but they had wives and families and that kept them pretty busy. What I really missed were women. I wasn't looking for a romantic relationship so much as I just wanted a female friend. Where I worked was almost exclusively men and I had next to zero contact with the few women that did work there. One evening after work, I prayed one of my "Oh God help!" prayers and asked God for a woman friend.

Two or three days later, as I was coming home from work, I noticed a very cute young woman with the hood up on a junked out car. She was parked just a few spaces from my parking space. I *had* to help of course! Her name was Mary Beth. She told me the car had overheated, but after it had cooled down and she had put water in it, it drove home fine. I asked if she wanted me to look at it, but she said "No, it'll be okay. I'm getting a new car in a few weeks." It turned out that her apartment was back to back with mine. I told her if she had any more trouble just to knock on my door and I'd look at it for her. The knock at the door came later that evening. She told me the car had overheated and she'd walked back from about a mile away and asked if I could help.

After we got the car back to the apartments, I determined that the thermostat was stuck shut. She told me she didn't want to spend any money to fix it if she could help it, since she was getting a new car in a few weeks. So, I pulled the thermostat out and made a makeshift gasket using gasket cement. I told her that would work for a while, but it was somewhat like putting the car together with glue and rubber bands. As I looked at the engine, I quickly noticed a significant number of other problems. This car was on its last legs. She didn't want me to fix it. I told her it would be lucky to make it to the car lot to trade in. (She told me later that it died on the lot, and they had to tow it away.) For my trouble, Mary Beth cooked me a lasagna dinner. Nothing like a home cooked meal for a single man! I can cook, but would rather not.

About a week or two later, I came home from work on a Wednesday night to find Mary Beth sitting outside in her new 1984 Chrysler Laser. After the usual small talk, I asked her if she was going to give me a ride in her new car or not. She said "Sure, want to go to church?" I said okay and off we went. We went east about ten miles to a little town called Rockwall. The exit we turned off was in the middle of a cow pasture with a four-way stop at a two-lane road. I was amazed to see the police directing traffic. I had seen this once or twice at big churches in big cities on a Sunday, but never on a Wednesday and never in what seemed like the middle of nowhere. We came to a church that was just full of excitement and anticipation. It held over a thousand people and was full. After a very upbeat charismatic praise and worship service followed by some excellent preaching, the pastor made a call for visitors, asking if we would let them pray for them. I answered the call. When I came back, Mary Beth asked me what I thought about the service. My answer was "I'd come back. I got something out of that." So every Wednesday, Mary Beth came by and asked me to go to church. After a while, I began to go Sunday's also, and started making sure that she went also.

The church was called Church on the Rock and it was known for being a praying church. But I really didn't know how to pray. If I prayed at all, it was still "Oh God help" type of prayers. After I was there a few months, I was sitting on the second or third row off to one side on a Wednesday night, when the pastor, Dr. Larry Lea, paused in his preaching, turned in my general direction (though not noticing me) and said "...and then I got the revelation that the Lord's prayer was an outline". Something went off in me. Something said "that was it". I have no idea what the message was that night, but the message to me was "The Lord's prayer is an outline."

My previous experience was that it took about 17 seconds to say the Lord's Prayer, and then what? An outline was a different thing altogether. This was something I *had* to do. That very night I went home and prayed the Lord's prayer as an outline. I prayed for

45 minutes! I had an *experience* with God! I did it again the next night, and the next. The time increased. I soon realized that if I wanted to keep having this time with God, I would have to start getting up early in the morning to pray. It was too hard to fit it in otherwise. I started getting up an hour earlier and started skipping breakfast to pray. I've been doing it now for over 19 years. My Red Sea had just parted. I had no idea, but I was on my way to the promised land.

Questions for consideration or discussion

1. Have you had experiences in your life that just "seemed to work out" in spite of your best laid plans failing? Write these down or discuss them.
2. Have you prayed "Oh God help" prayers and actually seen some of them answered? Name a specific instance.
3. What is prayer to you?
4. When you pray, do you have a structure or balance to your prayer time? If so, describe.
5. Is praying more than a few minutes seem like drudgery for you? Why or why not?
6. Do you experience the presence of God in your prayer time? If so, how does this affect you?
7. Have you considered "The Lord's Prayer" as an outline for prayer, or just as "words to say"? Has your opinion changed after reading this chapter?
8. Are you willing to try praying "The Lord's Prayer" as an outline? Will you start today?

Chapter 3
More than Salvation, The Kingdom of God

And He sent them to preach the Kingdom of God, and to heal the sick. (Luke 9:2)

So what is this promised land anyway? The Bible calls it *"a good land and ..., unto a land flowing with milk and honey" (Exodus 3:8)*, and *"a land that floweth with milk and honey; as the LORD God of thy fathers hath promised thee" (Dueteronomy 27:3)*. So what has God promised us today as believers?

> *Behold, the days come, saith the LORD, that I will make a new covenant with the house of Israel, and with the house of Judah: Not according to the covenant that I made with their fathers in the day that I took them by the hand to bring them out of the land of Egypt; which my covenant they brake, although I was an husband unto them, saith the LORD: But this shall be the covenant that I will make with the house of Israel; After those days, saith the LORD, I will put my law in their inward parts, and write it in their hearts; and will be their God, and they shall be my people. (Jeremiah 31:31-33)*

First of all he promised a new covenant, where He would put the law in our hearts. Jesus said:

> *Think not that I am come to destroy the law, or the prophets: I am not come to destroy, but to fulfil. For verily I say unto you, Till heaven and earth pass, one jot or one tittle shall in no wise pass from the law, till all be fulfilled. (Matthew 5:17-18)*

15

Essentially, He promised that He would also fulfill the old covenant. The fulfillment of the old covenant, through Jesus, in the new covenant is our promise. I will cover more on the covenant promises of the old covenant later on. I have learned that this is truly summed up as the Kingdom of God. What is the Kingdom of God? It is a place (a promised land) where *everything* is provided.

Is this kingdom of God just for us in heaven someday, or is it also for here on earth? As I shared earlier, my upbringing made me to believe that the kingdom of God was in heaven and I was to do the best I could here on earth. What does the Bible have to say about this?

> *When Jesus saw that he had answered wisely, He said to him, "You are not far from the kingdom of God." (Mark 12:34)*
> (Jesus giving instructions to His disciples) *Heal the sick who are there and tell them, "The Kingdom of God is near you" (Luke 10: 9)*

Notice, He is not saying "You are about to die"... So, clearly the Kingdom of God is for earth. Also, in the Lord's Prayer the Lord instructs us to pray:

> *Thy Kingdom come, Thy will be done, on earth as it is in heaven. (Matthew 6:10)*

So God asks us to pray for the kingdom of heaven on earth.

> *And this is the confidence that we have in him, that, if we ask any thing according to his will, he heareth us: And if we know that he hear us, whatsoever we ask, we know that we have the petitions that we desired of him. (1 John 5:14-15)*

So God not only asks us to pray for His kingdom on earth, but promises us that if we do, we will have His kingdom on earth as it is in heaven.

I have heard it said something to the effect of "I'm saved, therefore I am in the kingdom of God." If that was true, I should have been in the kingdom of God already. I believed that Jesus had died for my sins and had assurance that I would go to heaven because of that, and not because of my works, were I to die. This is saved, but it is surely not the kingdom of God! My life was not much different from the rest of the people in the world who were not saved. So there must be more. In 1 Tim 2:4 it says (God) *"Who wants all men to be saved **and** come to a knowledge of the truth"* (emphasis added). Coming to the "knowledge of the truth" is separate and distinct from, and subsequent to salvation. There is something more than salvation. There is the kingdom of God.

So what is the kingdom of God on earth? Romans 14:17 states *"For the Kingdom of God is not a matter of eating and drinking, but of righteousness, peace and joy in the Holy Spirit."* Do you walk in righteousness daily? Is there peace in every circumstance? Is there an inner joy no matter what happens? If you lose your job and have nothing to fall back on, does your world fall apart? This happened to me. I can't say it was easy, but I had learned much about living in the kingdom of God by that time. I had real peace. I had an inner joy. When the terrorist attacks hit America, did it change your life? Do you worry? The kingdom of God is a place where these things won't move you.

1 Corinthians 4:20 states *"For the Kingdom of God is not a matter of talk, but of power."* What kind of power? The power to be a son of God. How do we receive this kingdom in our lives? That is the entire subject of this book, but I will summarize it briefly

here. In Luke 18:17 Jesus said *"I tell you the truth, Anyone who will not receive the kingdom of God like a little child will never enter it."* We have already ascertained that the reference to the kingdom of God here is not only to that in heaven, but also on earth. What is unique about a little child? A little child *trusts* in his father for *everything*, not worrying. In a good family, with a good father, have you ever heard a child worry about whether they would have anything to eat that day? Or worry about if they would have clothes to wear, or a place to live? God is a good father, better than the best of our earthly fathers (Mark 10:18). God's family is a good family, better than the best of our earthly families.

So we want to be a "son of God" and trust our heavenly Father. Did we get that with salvation? I think if you ask most Christians, they would say "I'm saved, therefore I'm a son of God". But what do the scriptures say?

> *For as many as are **led** by the Spirit of God, they are the sons of God (Rom 8:14)*
> *But as many as received Him, to them gave he **power** to become the sons of God, even to them that believe on His name* (John 1:12 emphasis added).

We know that if we receive Him, we are saved. It gives us power to become a son of God. We already showed that the kingdom of God is about power. So we need to "become a son" and *trust* in God. To trust Him for everything is to live in the kingdom of God. (Yes it is true that when we are first saved we *"receive the adoption of sons"* (Galatians 4:5). However, this is as a new babe in Christ and *"the heir, as long as he is a child, differeth nothing from a servant, though he be lord of all"* (Galatians 4:1). I am speaking of being a "mature in Christ" son of God. We cannot inherit the fullness of the kingdom of God as an immature believer.)

To trust Him, we must know Him. We can't trust someone we don't know, but only know about. For example, as I write this, Bill Gates, founder of Microsoft is considered the richest man in the world. Almost everyone, at least in America, has heard of him. Imagine if one day your phone rang, and a voice on the other end of the line said "I'm Bill Gate's secretary, and I'm calling to tell you that Bill said he was going to pay off all your debts, buy you a big new house, and give you a yearly income of $100,000 for the rest of your life." I can tell you that you would not believe it. You would hope it was true, but you sure weren't about to quit your job based on that phone call. However, if Bill Gates was your uncle, and you had spent much time with him, and developed a real relationship with him, your response would be much different, because you would know him. How much more are we able to trust in a loving God if we know Him!

So, how do we get to know God? First, we must be saved. In John 3:3 Jesus said *"I tell you the truth, no one can see the kingdom of god unless his is born again"*. If you are not sure of your salvation, it is time to give your heart to Jesus. Start by saying this prayer to God from your heart:

> God in heaven, I come to you in the name of Jesus. I believe Jesus died for my sins, and on the third day he rose from the dead. I turn from my sins and I turn to you. Come into my heart and be the Lord of my life. I give my life to you.

Second, we must continue in the Word. Jesus said in John 8:31 and 32, *"If you continue in my word, then you are my disciples indeed, and you shall know the truth and the truth shall make you free."* Recall that in 1 Timothy 2:4 the Bible states that God *"wants all men to be saved and come to a knowledge of the truth."* This truth will make us free. Free to trust in God for everything. Free to live in the kingdom of God.

Finally, we must spend time with God. It is impossible to know someone unless you spend time with them. They may be your acquaintance. You may have met them. However, until you spend time with them, you will not know them.

How do we spend time with God? We must start by putting God first. In Matthew 6:33, Jesus said *"Seek ye first the kingdom of God, and His righteousness, and all these other things shall be added unto you."* He put God first, and all other things afterwards. We do this in two ways, praise and prayer. When we praise God, He inhabits our praises. *"But Thou are holy, oh thou that inhabits the praises of Israel."* (Psalm 22:3) When we pray, we spend time with God.

The Lord's prayer (Matthew 6:9 and following) is all about the kingdom of God. The first words of the prayer are "Father in heaven". We want to be sons of God. We praise him as Father, and He inhabits our praise. When I had been praying through the Lord's Prayer as an outline for a couple of months, the reality of God as my Father hit home. I was praying and I said to God, "God in heaven, you really *are* my Father."

God then spoke to me, as clear as any word I ever heard before or since and said to me "And you are my son." It moved me to tears, joyful tears. For the first time I had some concept of God's love for me. I could relate because of how much I loved my own sons, and how much I would give for them. It was a life changing moment.

The second verse of the prayer is *"Hallowed be thy name"*. The word "hallowed" means "let be sanctified, be holy". This didn't mean a lot to me. After praying this prayer for many years I have a definition that is more easily grasped. In my words this verse means to hold God's name in the highest reverence, set apart from worldly things, above all else. Yes, that means sanctified and holy, but this definition works better for me. It is a form of praise and reverence for God.

What name do we hallow? God, Jesus, or many of the other names for God? I have a book on the names of God that has well over 100 different names for God in the Bible. All of these are good, but why not put a focus on the covenant names of God? Jesus came to fulfill the old covenant. Proverbs 18:10 states *"The name of the Lord is a strong tower, the righteous runneth into it and is safe."* Why is the name a strong tower? Because it is a covenant name. God does not break His covenants.

Exodus 3:14 and 15 states *"And God said unto Moses, I AM THAT I AM: and he said, Thus shalt thou say unto the children of Israel, I AM hath sent me unto you. And God said moreover unto Moses, Thus shalt thou say unto the children of Israel, The LORD God of your fathers, the God of Abraham, the God of Isaac, and the God of Jacob, hath sent me unto you: this is my name for ever, and this is my memorial unto all generations."* The Hebrew here for I AM is Yahweh or Jehovah, and it is His name forever. It is compounded in Hebrew with eight different names or attributes of God and these are His names forever. His compound names are:

The Lord our Righteousness (Jehovah-tsidkenu): Jeremiah 23:6 ... *this is his name whereby he shall be* called, THE LORD OUR RIGHTEOUSNESS.

The Lord our Sanctification (Jehovah-m'kaddesh): Leviticus 20:8 *I am the LORD which sanctify you.* Exodus 31:13 *I am the LORD that doth sanctify you.*

The Lord our Peace (Jehovah-shalom) Judges 6:24 *Then Gideon built an altar there unto the LORD, and called it Jehovahshalom*

The Lord Who is Present (Jehovah-shammah) Ezekiel 48:35 *The name of the city from that day shall be, The LORD is there.*

The Lord our Healer (Jehovah-rophe) Exodus 15:26 *For I am the LORD that healeth thee.*

The Lord our Provider (Jehovah-jireh) Genesis 22:14 *And Abraham called the name of that place Jehovahjireh: as it is said to this day, In the mount of the LORD it shall be seen.*

The Lord our Banner (Jehovah-nissi) Exodus 17:15 *And Moses built an altar, and called the name of it Jehovahnissi*

The Lord our Shepherd (Jehovah-rohi) Psalms 23:1 *The LORD is my shepherd*

Encompassed in these names of God is every need in your life. God fulfilled these covenant names through Jesus and gave them to us through his sacrifice on the cross. As we hallow His names, His covenant names, He will inhabit our praise and we will begin to know Him as He says that He is. The next eight chapters will give you an example of what this really means relative to the covenant names of God.

Questions for consideration or discussion

1.   Have you received Jesus Christ as your Lord and Savior, placing your entire trust for your eternal salvation in Him? If not, why not? Are you ready to do so now?

2.   Do you call God Father? If so, is this real to you, or just a statement that you find in the bible? Why or why not?

3.   Have you considered yourself to be a son (or daughter) of God? What do you think after reading this chapter? What step are you ready to take to further your position as a son?

4.   When you consider the kingdom of God, do you think of it in terms of being near you, or as being far off, or in heaven, or for today or just for someday in eternity? Explain.

5.   Can you honestly say that you trust in God for everything in your life? Or are their areas that you look to yourself, your job, your doctor, your parents, your government, etc.? Expound on this.

6.   Do you have a real knowledge of who God is based on who His word says He is in the eight covenant names discussed in this chapter? State a personal testimony for each one (if you can).

Chapter 4
Righteousness by Faith, Faith by Hearing
The Lord Our Righteousness

He leadeth me in the paths of righteousness for his name's sake (Psalm 23:3)

I was a person who did not want anything to do with "religion". I still am this way today. Now let me clarify what I mean by "religion". The Bible calls this *"dead works"* (Hebrews 6:1). These are things that we do with the intent to make us approved to God, or in some cases, approved by men. Isaiah 64:6 says *"All our righteousnesses are as filthy rags."* Our righteousness is in Christ alone. Romans 3:22 states *"The righteousness of God which is by faith of Jesus Christ unto all and upon all them that believe."* So the entirety of our righteousness is through the cross. No work that we do will make us any more righteous than just having faith in Jesus Christ. Most believers understand this well when they get saved. Then the first thing that happens is some well-meaning believers start giving them the rules to live by. Some of the more common ones are "don't drink", "don't cuss", "don't smoke" and the list goes on. It is not that these statements are necessarily wrong, but it is not our responsibility to tell people their sins. The responsibility to convict of sins belongs to the Holy Spirit. John 16:7 and 8 state *"Unless I go away, the Counselor will not come to you; but if I go, I will send him to you. When he comes, he will convict the world of guilt in regard to sin and righteousness and judgment." (NIV)*

This generally goes beyond trying to be saved by works, but rather, it is an attempt to be perfected by works. Even the apostle Peter had this problem.

But when Peter was come to Antioch, I withstood him to the face, because he was to be blamed. For before that certain came from James, he did eat with the Gentiles: but when they were come, he withdrew and separated himself, fearing them which were of the circumcision. And the other Jews dissembled likewise with him; insomuch that Barnabas also was carried away with their dissimulation. But when I saw that they walked not uprightly according to the truth of the gospel, I said unto Peter before them all, If thou, being a Jew, livest after the manner of Gentiles, and not as do the Jews, why compellest thou the Gentiles to live as do the Jews? (Galatians 2:11-14)

The apostle Paul continued in his letter to the Galatians and said *"O foolish Galatians, who hath bewitched you, that ye should not obey the truth"* (Galatians 3:1) and *"Are ye so foolish? having begun in the Spirit, are ye now made perfect by the flesh?"* (Galatians 3:3)

Do you find yourself struggling to measure up to some level that you told yourself was how good you needed to be? Or, as above, well-meaning Christians have given you a list of rules to live by and you find you can't do it. For these rules are powerless to change us. *"For what the law could not do, in that it was weak through the flesh, God sending his own Son in the likeness of sinful flesh, and for sin, condemned sin in the flesh: That the righteousness of the law might be fulfilled in us, who walk not after the flesh, but after the Spirit."* (Romans 8:3,4) To be free from sin, we must *"Walk in the Spirit, and ye shall not fulfil the lust of the flesh."* (Galatians 5:16). Rules such as these condemn us. When we walk in the spirit, *"There is therefore now no condemnation to them which are in Christ Jesus, who walk not after the flesh, but after the Spirit."* (Romans 8:1) When you find yourself in condemnation, rebuke condemnation and quote that scripture. When you find yourself convicted of sin, turn to God and repent.

A related thing that can happen with well-meaning Christians is they get wrapped up in too many works. James 2:26 states *"For as the body without the spirit is dead, so faith without works is dead also."* As you can see, there is a scriptural basis for works. We should have works of faith. However, there is a point where this goes over the line. Our works today are generally not in attempting to observe the law, but rather in serving the church. So where do we draw the line? The book of 1 Samuel gives us the answer.

> *And the LORD sent thee on a journey, and said, Go and utterly destroy the sinners the Amalekites, and fight against them until they be consumed. Wherefore then didst thou not obey the voice of the LORD, but didst fly upon the spoil, and didst evil in the sight of the LORD? And Saul said unto Samuel, Yea, I have obeyed the voice of the LORD, and have gone the way which the LORD sent me, and have brought Agag the king of Amalek, and have utterly destroyed the Amalekites. But the people took of the spoil, sheep and oxen, the chief of the things which should have been utterly destroyed, to sacrifice unto the LORD thy God in Gilgal. And Samuel said, Hath the LORD as great delight in burnt offerings and sacrifices, as in obeying the voice of the LORD? Behold, to obey*

is better than sacrifice, and to hearken
than the fat of rams. (1 Samuel 15:18-
22)

What works should we do and what works are effectively dead works? We need to do works of obedience. To obey God in our works, we have to hear from God so that He may direct us. He alone is the Lord our Righteousness. What Saul had done was save *"the best of the sheep and of the oxen, to sacrifice unto the LORD thy God"* (1 Samuel 15:15) Sacrifices and offerings were scripturally sound. They were "good works". However, they were in direct conflict with God's spoken word to Saul through the prophet Samuel.

When I was living in Garland, Texas, east of Dallas, I was interested in joining a newly forming Dallas chapter of a group called "The Fellowship of Christian Musicians and Artists". I really wasn't sure God had called me to join this group, but I was definitely interested. The first meeting of that group was going to be in Fort Worth, forty or fifty miles away, through some bad traffic. The day of the meeting had been a rough day at work, and I had to drive over 30 miles home from my Lewisville office along LBJ freeway, the worst traffic in Dallas. On the way home, I had said to God, "Lord, I'm not sure if you want me to be part of this group or not. I'm tired and don't really want to drive all the way to Fort Worth. If you want me to go, tell me the scripture, chapter and verse, in the book of Revelation that talks about where the angels are given the trumpets." By the time I got home, I was tired. I did not feel like going. I had forgotten about my fleece to God on whether I was to go or not. I sat down and picked up my Bible to read it. The Spirit of God quickened to me to read Revelation 8:2 which states *"And I saw the seven angels which stood before God; and to them were given seven trumpets."* As soon as I read the verse I remembered the prayer I had prayed. I knew it was God's will for me to go. I had a decision to make. I could stay home and read my Bible. This would have been a good work. Or I could get up and drive to Fort Worth. I'm happy to say that I chose the long drive to Fort Worth. I chose obedience, which in this case, I also considered a sacrifice.

Have you ever participated in a church activity or ministry that was absolutely a "good thing"? However, as you were involved in it, it became a major burden. It didn't work with your family. You seemed to be cutting short your time in prayer, or with your family. Your priorities seemed to get out of line. There seemed to be no grace with your husband or wife as to the requirements of that ministry. You knew it was important. You knew it was a good thing. Somehow, no one else in your family could see it. They only saw you putting it ahead of them. In this case, consider the possibility that God did not call you to that ministry, but you may have called yourself. You may have made an altar of cut stones. Deuteronomy 27:5 states *"And there shalt thou build an altar unto the LORD thy God, an altar of stones: thou shalt not lift up any iron tool upon them."* You may have put your efforts into something God did not call you to. If He has ordained the ministry, He has also called people to do it. Remember Jesus said *"For my yoke is easy, and my burden is light."* (Matthew 11:30) So, there is a yoke, which is work, but with the anointing and calling of God, the burden is light. This calls for prayer, and hearing from God.

The church I began to attend had a new member's class called "Finding the Rock". Although I began to consider myself a member, I did not initially sign up to take the class, although I actually ended up attending probably half or more of the classes at one

28

point. However, I had an issue with what I considered to be man-made rules. As I stated, I was greatly opposed to religion. I did not want man-made rules and requirements. At that time, I had no understanding of proper spiritual authority. In my opinion, the required class was nothing more than a man-made rule. A number of people came and told me I should take the class. I listened, somewhat anyway, and then proceeded to ignore them. However, every day I continued to pray *"Thy kingdom come. Thy will be done, on earth as it is in heaven."* (Matthew 6:10) I prayed that with all my heart, and really meant it. During that time, I worked for Texas Instruments, and one of the things I often did in my job was to redline blueprints, often crossing things out. God gave me a dream one night. In my dream was the blueprint of my life, and I was crossing out a note on the blueprint marked "Jesus Christ Fundamentation". I woke up and immediately knew that I was wrong. God was speaking to me, and I needed to take the class. I immediately signed up and took the class, and every follow-on class they offered.

Many people struggle with the idea of hearing God speak. As I grew up, this was not something that I had ever even heard of. However, it is absolutely essential to understanding how to *"live and move and have your being"* (Acts 17:28) in the kingdom of God. The Bible is very clear that God does in fact speak to his people. *"My sheep hear my voice, and I know them, and they follow me."* (John 10:27)

God speaks to his people in many ways. First, He speaks to us through his written word. Most Christians don't have a problem with that statement. He speaks to us in dreams and visions. Joel 2:28 and Acts 2:17 both state *"In the last days, saith God, I will pour out of my Spirit upon all flesh: and your sons and your daughters shall prophesy, and your young men shall see visions, and your old men shall dream dreams."* Peter's statement in Acts 2:16 also showed that the last days started at Pentecost. So we are still in the last days. Ever tell someone you had a dream or saw a vision from God? In most Christian churches in America, this is enough for them to consider you out of your mind (at best).

There are times that you know that you know that you know that God is "speaking" to you, but you never heard a voice. You just know. An example of this is Acts 16:6 *"Now when they had gone throughout Phrygia and the region of Galatia, and were forbidden of the Holy Ghost to preach the word in Asia".* In this case, it is a work of the Holy Spirit working in your spirit to lead you and guide you. Finally, God speaks to us in a *"still small voice"* as shown in 1 Kings 19:12 and 13 *"And after the earthquake a fire; but the LORD was not in the fire: and after the fire a still small voice. And it was so, when Elijah heard it, that he wrapped his face in his mantle, and went out, and stood in the entering in of the cave. And, behold, there came a voice unto him, and said, What doest thou here, Elijah?"* I've heard the excuse that Elijah was an old testament prophet and that God doesn't speak to today's believer that way, since we have the written word. However, a New Testament example of this is Acts 8:29 *"Then the Spirit said unto Philip, Go near, and join thyself to this chariot."* Now Philip was definitely a man of God, but the Bible does not call him an apostle or prophet. It calls him a man of honest report, full of the Holy Spirit and wisdom, who was chosen as one of seven to oversee the daily distribution of food to widows (see Acts 6:1-6). So, the Bible shows that God even speaks to the "common" man, not just his apostles and prophets. Here is one more example. In Acts 9:10-16 God speaks to a man named Ananias as follows:

And there was a certain disciple at Damascus, named Ananias; and to him said the Lord in a vision, Ananias. And he said, Behold, I am here, Lord. And the Lord said unto him, Arise, and go into the street which is called Straight, and enquire in the house of Judas for one called Saul, of Tarsus: for, behold, he prayeth, And hath seen in a vision a man named Ananias coming in, and putting his hand on him, that he might receive his sight. Then Ananias answered, Lord, I have heard by many of this man, how much evil he hath done to thy saints at Jerusalem: And here he hath authority from the chief priests to bind all that call on thy name. But the Lord said unto him, Go thy way: for he is a chosen vessel unto me, to bear my name before the Gentiles, and kings, and the children of Israel: For I will shew him how great things he must suffer for my name's sake.

In this case Ananias is not a prophet or apostle. He is just called a disciple, which is a follower of Jesus.

The next argument I've heard against this is that "That was in the early days of the church. They didn't have the Bible then". First of all, they did have the entire Old Testament. Secondly, it conflicts with John 10:27 shown above, Hebrews 13:8 *"Jesus Christ the same yesterday, and today, and forever"* and Malachi 3:6 *"I am the LORD, I change not."* As you can see, God speaks to his people all throughout the Bible, old and new testaments. He changes not. Therefore, He continues to speak to his people today.

When God spoke to me through that dream that woke me up, I learned something. Actually, I had learned a lot of things. I not only learned specifically what God's will was relative to taking the class. I also learned that God gave authority to the leaders in His church. This does not always mean that they are right, but it does mean that we should be submitted to them in the requirements that they place upon membership, leadership, eldership, etc. in the church. If you can't submit to these requirements, then you are in the wrong church.

This is true no matter what church you are in. As I shared earlier, I came from a devout Catholic family. My father died of a heart attack when I was 18 years old. My mother lived as a widow for quite a number of years after that. Eventually, my mother met a man who wanted to marry her. This man was not a Catholic. He was also a divorced man. The Catholic Church has very specific rules and requirements relative to marrying outside of the Catholic Church and particularly about marrying someone who has been divorced. It takes approval from the church authorities in Rome. Sometimes this approval is very long in coming.

My mother, being a good Catholic, chose to submit her potential marriage to the Catholic Church for approval. After about two years, this approval was still pending. Friends, and possibly even family, were suggesting that she just get married and then the approval would come. Apparently, that is what most people in the Catholic Church do in this situation, and supposedly it speeds up the approval. One day, I was talking to my mother on the phone and she asked my opinion of this. My response was that if she wanted to be a member of the Catholic Church, she should be submitted to its rules. Otherwise, she needed to be in a church where she could submit to their requirements. To be honest, I was a bit surprised that my mother asked me this question as I was the only one in our family that attended a church other than the Catholic Church. I never asked her, but I suspect that she was surprised at my answer. My mother waited for the approval of the church.

Probably the most important thing I learned when God spoke to me is that I won't miss knowing God's will for my life. If I sincerely seek God for his will and pray for it daily. He will make sure that I know what it is. I can still choose to ignore it and do my own thing, which I am personally determined not to do, but God will make sure I know his will. In my case, to this day, I continue to be "slow" to act on "works". I want to be sure that I'm doing what God desires for me and not too much. I believe strongly that every church member has a place to serve in and through their local church. I also know that if we submit to God, He will show us exactly where He wants us to serve. When we do this, we can *"enter into his rest"* (Hebrews 3:18). There will be grace and anointing for that which God has called us to do. There will be time for family, time for work, time for church, and time for ministry. It may be a lot of work, but it will not be a heavy burden. Jesus said *"For my yoke is easy, and my burden is light."* (Matthew 11:30).

So the righteousness that we desire is by faith, not of works. *"But to him that worketh not, but believeth on him that justifieth the ungodly, his faith is counted for righteousness."* (Romans 4:5) Yet we serve as servants of righteousness. *"Being then made free from sin, ye became the servants of righteousness."* (Romans 6:18) This faith that produces righteousness, and works of righteousness, comes by hearing God speak. *"So then faith cometh by hearing, and hearing by the word of God."* (Romans 10:17) Note that this reference to the word of God in Romans 10:17 is specifically to the spoken word of God (rhema in Greek). And *"The just shall live by*

33

faith." (Romans 1:17) could almost be written as "the just shall live by faith that comes from hearing God speak", since that is where faith comes from. Unless we hear from God, our righteousness will only be of works and shall not exceed that of the Old Testament scribes and Pharisees. And we cannot enter the kingdom of heaven. *"Except your righteousness shall exceed the righteousness of the scribes and Pharisees, ye shall in no case enter into the kingdom of heaven."* (Matthew 5:20)

Questions for consideration or discussion

1. When you look at your life, are you living by rules or being led by the Spirit? Explain.

2. Are you serving in your local church? If not, have you considered asking God where you should be serving? Why or why not?

3. Are there things you are "doing for the Lord" that just seem to be an undue burden? Are they adversely affecting you prayer time, family life, health etc.? If so, what will you do different?

4. Do you hear from God? If so, how do you hear from Him? Do you "just know that you know", have dreams or visions, or possibly hear the still small voice? How do you know that the voice that you hear is from God? Does it bring peace or confusion? (It should bring peace.)

5. Are you concerned about knowing "for sure" what God is speaking to you, or His direction for you? Are you praying "Your kingdom come and Your will be done, on earth as it is in heaven" every day? Are you praying this over your decisions? Consider your last major decisions. How did you make them?

Chapter 5
From Glory to Glory
The Lord Our Sanctification

*Wherefore come out from among them, and be ye
separate, saith the Lord, and touch not the unclean
thing; and I will receive you (2 Corinthians 6:17)*

God's word says *"Be ye holy; for I am holy"* (1
Peter 1:16). How do we know what holiness is? How
do we achieve this? We just showed that our
righteousness is not a set of rules. It follows that our
sanctification cannot be either. Yet the command is for
us to be holy. It clearly infers an act of our will,
something that we must choose to do. However,
without holiness, no man shall see God. Hebrews
12:14 states *"Follow peace with all men, and holiness,
without which no man shall see the Lord"*. If seeing
the Lord depends on our holiness, and we have to do it,
we are in trouble. Not one of us can be holy on our
own. We need the Lord to sanctify us and set us apart
from this world and apart from our sin.

As I began to really seek the Lord in prayer,
many things began to drop out of my life. Much of
these were because I didn't have time for them
anymore. Others were because I didn't have a heart for
them anymore. As part of this, at times it seemed I had
given up something. This included, to some extent, my
friends. Not that I had rejected them, or they rejected
me, but rather that I was into a new life and they were
still in the old life. I didn't become too good for them.
It was more that I had moved on. When I saw these old
friends it was with a burning desire for them to
understand the new life I had, and that they could have
it too.

Once, I was taking a class on statistical process
controls required by my job at Texas Instruments. The

class was in a hotel conference room away from the company location, and away from the day to day. There were quite a few of my coworkers in the class. I got along okay with them, but there was no real interaction other than that required by work. We worked in the same division, but rarely very close. After the class one day, I overheard one of the men inviting others to go out to "happy hour". I didn't really want to go to happy hour, but I found myself wanting to be invited and included, which I was not. In my heart I shared this with God. His answer to me was a rebuke, firm, but loving. Essentially the word was *"Set your affection on things above, not on things on the earth."* (Colossians 3:2) This was probably not the exact words, but it was essentially the meaning. It both was and wasn't the answer I wanted to hear. The desire to be included didn't go away (at least not at that time), but the desire to follow God's leading in my life was stronger. The Lord had set me apart. I was not going to make a decision to go against His work.

In 1986, I traveled to my home town, Bowie, Maryland, to visit with my sister Marguerite and attend my High School reunion. During my visit, I shared some of what God had been doing in my life with my sister and her husband. I ran into what I considered a solid wall of resistance, even though all I was doing was relating some of the changes in my life. I wasn't pushing them at all, at least I didn't think so, and still don't today. Eventually, I found out why. My sister shared with me a story of someone whom they had considered a friend that came to them to tell them he had been born again. Unfortunately, it didn't stop there. Apparently, this friend didn't just tell them what had happened to him, but he also told them that they couldn't be his friend any more, since they weren't born again also. Sounds like someone gave him a set of rules on how to be a Christian and he was doing his best to follow them. I could easily understand why my sister was not very receptive.

Usually, when we just begin to really serve the Lord, there are people in our life that just aren't good for us, and we are not really in a position or place where we are likely to turn them to the ways of God. We don't usually know it, but God does. When I moved to the Dallas area, music was a pretty big part of my life. It didn't take long to link up with other musicians and we became an informal band. There were 2 other keyboard players (in addition to me), so I generally played guitar, a bass player, and a couple of vocalists. We would get together on a semi-regular basis to jam and record. None of these were bad people. Most I met through my job. They weren't into drugs or any bad things, but they weren't Christians either. This was something I really enjoyed doing and it seemed pretty harmless to me. They knew I had begun to attend church regularly, but other than that, nothing really changed at first. Then things started happening where we couldn't get together. First, the bass player had personal problems and couldn't come regularly. Eventually, these things forced him to move to Oklahoma. Next, one of the keyboard players began to have conflicts with family requirements and couldn't come. Shortly thereafter, the other keyboard player, took a new job and moved to California. Needless to say, there was no more band. The Lord had separated me from this, which I now realize really wasn't good for my Christian walk. I had a choice to make. I could have found another bass player, another keyboard player or guitarist and so on, or I could trust God. God filled up my life with many other things where I no longer missed the band. My music began to change from secular music to Christian music.

Not only did my music change to Christian music, my listening habits changed to Christian music.

Fortunately, in the Dallas area there was an excellent contemporary Christian music station. Growing up, the only Christian music I ever heard was at church. Primarily the music was old hymns, choir songs and the like. The most modern music I ever heard in church was the folk mass music, which was led by musicians with folk guitars. None of this was on the radio. I listened to the same music everyone else my age listened to. I played in rock and roll bands and played the top forty music. In the 1983 time frame, living in Bremerton Washington, I heard a Seattle Christian radio station, on the FM dial, playing contemporary Christian music for the first time. I found myself tuning to this station occasionally. Unfortunately, they would regularly play old hymns, which I found boring and I'd change the station. Prior to this time I never even knew that this type of music existed. It intrigued me. I even tried to write a Christian song once. It was a dud. I didn't know enough about God to even start.

As my music changed, I had quit listening to all my old record albums. I had begun to purchase some Christian music albums, and this is what I listened to if I wasn't listening to the radio. I loved those old albums, but they just sat on the shelf. The music on them was the best of what I had grown up with, from the 60's and 70's mostly. I had known people in high school that would have been very envious of the record collection I had. These were not "satanic" music albums, but more like the kind of music you would hear on an "oldie's" station today. When I first began to pray regularly, probably about a year earlier, the Holy Spirit had revealed to me one of my albums was by an artist who was pushing satanic stuff. I had immediately pulled this out and destroyed it on the spot. The remaining albums had no such evil message. They were just secular music. Attached to them were lots of old memories. As I sought the Lord, one day, I felt strongly that the Lord was telling me to get rid of them. I really didn't understand this, and it was a hard thing to do. I didn't listen to them anymore, but I really didn't want to get rid of them. The Lord confirmed his word to me with a scripture. *"All things are lawful unto me, but all things are not expedient"* (1 Corinthians 6:12 and 10:23) I boxed them up and made plans to take them to a used record store. Before I had managed to offload these albums, I shared what I felt the Lord had said to me with my friend Harriet. She hit the nail on the head when she said to me that the Lord was cleaning out my past. I then understood. Much more than getting rid of the music, I was getting rid of the past and the memories, both good and bad, that went with it. This put a fire in me to get them out fast.

After I had gotten rid of all these albums, while I was praying, I told the Lord I had done what He asked. A most glorious thing happened. God showed me His glory! For a split second I "saw" in my spirit, not with my natural eyes, His holiness, His glory! It was awesome! It was powerful! It was pure! It was like nothing I have ever experienced before or since. It was life changing! I went through everything I owned. If there was anything that I felt didn't line up with the holiness of God I had seen, I cleaned it out and got rid of it. The glimpse I saw couldn't have been for more than one second, and was probably considerably less. The impact it had on my life continues today. I still judge everything by that revelation. I have asked God more than once to let me see it again, to no avail. I know that I will one day see God's glory again, and live in it forever. This is a day that I greatly look forward to. I suspect that if I saw much more of His glory, I could not live in the flesh or on this earth. Nothing compares. The Bible says *"Beloved, now are we the sons of God, and it doth not yet appear what we shall be: but we know that, when he shall appear, we shall be like him; for we shall see him as he is."* (1 John 3:2) What an awesome statement! When we see Him, we will be like Him. *"In a moment, in the twinkling of an eye, at the last trump: for the trumpet shall sound, and the dead shall be raised incorruptible, and we shall be changed."* (1 Corinthians 15:52) How I long for that day! For now, I can still "see" Him, if just a bit, in my praise and worship time. In that time of prayer where I hallow His name, I see Him today *"with open face beholding as in a glass the glory of the Lord"* (2 Corinthians 3:18) and I am *"changed into the same image from glory to glory, even as by the Spirit of the Lord"* (2 Corinthians 3:18) Daily, I am being *"conformed to the image of his Son"* (Romans 8:29).

"But ye are a chosen generation, a royal priesthood, an holy nation, a peculiar people; that ye should shew forth the praises of him who hath called you out of darkness into his marvellous light" (1 Peter 2:9)

Coming out from the world does not mean leaving the world, but it does mean to be different from the world. This includes not only in our actions, what we do and don't do, but it means learning the ways of God, and learning to walk in His ways. Sometimes this seems totally alien to this world. I have heard it said that "God works in mysterious ways." There is even a popular Christian song that says this. However, it really is not scriptural. These ways are only mysterious to the world. We are His disciples and we are to know the mystery of the kingdom of God. Matthew 13:11 says *"It is given unto you to know the mysteries of the kingdom of heaven."* (See also Mark 4:11 and Luke 8:10). In Isaiah 55:8 and 9 the Bible states *"For my thoughts are not your thoughts, neither are your ways my ways, saith the LORD. For as the heavens are higher than the earth, so are my ways higher than your ways, and my thoughts than your thoughts."* This was a rebuke to God's people as the prophet Isaiah encouraged them to seek the Lord and to repent. (See Isaiah 55:6 and 7) We are to know His ways.

Sometimes this means to do things in ways that don't make sense and are often contrary to what the world, or even the church, thinks is the thing to do. Let me give you an example of how different God's ways can be than our own ways. After being single again for about three or four years, I realized I didn't really like being single. I had done a little bit of dating after moving to the Dallas area, but it never really went anywhere. Fairly quickly after beginning to pray regularly, I realized that dating was probably not what God really wanted for me, at least for the time being. I assumed this was just for a season. However, time passed and I found I really wanted to get married again. One thing I really wanted to be sure of was that I didn't make another mistake. I wanted to marry the right woman. The right woman had to be God's plan for me. However, I just did not feel that it was God's will for me to date. This was somewhat of a paradox for me.

At that time, I was reading a book by Dr. Paul Y. Cho. One of the key messages in that book was to not just ask God generically for what you want or need, but to ask specifically. There was a testimony in the book about a woman who had been praying for a husband for many years to no avail. After counseling with Dr. Cho, he advised her to make a list of ten specific things she wanted in a husband, and then ask God for that. She met her husband and they married in just a few months. I decided that I would do the same. I made a list of ten things I wanted in my wife. I was very practical. Having been married before, I knew to ask for things that were really important. I can't say that I met and married my wife in a few months, but I do have a rather amazing story.

For a couple of years I worked with and taught children's choir at my church. As this season came to an end, the music pastor called for volunteers for a planned 24 hour praise and worship ministry. I felt a call to this and asked the Lord what time slot to sign up for. It seemed to me that the Lord's direction was for 6 AM to 8 AM on Saturday mornings. My natural response was "ugh". This was the only day of the week that I could sleep late. But if it was God's will, I would do it. When the list came around to sign up, there was no 6-8 AM time slot. The closest thing was as 5-7 AM slot. (It turned out that there was another list with a 6-8 AM time slot, but I never saw that list. Apparently, these lists were set up to provide for an overlap.) So I signed up for 5-7 AM on Saturday mornings. Saturday's became a very early day for me. I would get up at 3 AM, shower, shave, etc. and then pray for an hour before going to the church to lead praise and worship. It only took a few weeks before whoever had signed up for the 6-8 AM time slot to drop out. I don't even remember anyone on the 4-6 AM time slot. Three to five AM was covered by a husband and wife team I knew (Mike and Margie) and I would take over at 5 AM and continue until 8 AM when someone else came in to take over.

Some days there would be a pretty good number of people that would show up for praise and worship in this time slot. Other days it would just be me alone worshiping God for the entire three hours. One morning I showed up at 5 AM as usual, and for some reason, Mike and Margie weren't there. This was rather unusual, since they were very faithful. At the altar area in prayer was a man I did not know. Other than that, the place was empty. I went to the piano and began to praise and worship. This man joined in. Over the next hour or so, a number of other people showed up. One of these was my friend Harriet. This was a friendship God had ordained. Harriet is a sweet black woman a few years older than I. We had met working together in the children's choir ministry. The only thing we really have in common is Jesus. However, we had developed a good friendship over a couple of years.

During this time of worship, she introduced herself to the man, a church member, who had been praying when I arrived. As 8 AM arrived I also was introduced to him. His name was Sean. After talking a few minutes I invited him to join Harriet and I and one or two others for breakfast at Denny's. During breakfast he told us the story of how he had ended up there that morning. He had been out late. I think he said he'd been at a Christian music concert, that Friday night. On his way home that night around 2 AM or so, he felt that the Lord had told him to go to the church and pray and God would "meet him there". He told us that as soon as I started to play the piano, the presence of God hit him, and in his words "it was awesome". Thus we got to know Sean a bit.

Sunday evening, I attended the service at church and sat with Harriet. At the end of the service, Harriet said to me something similar to "There's Sean. I need to go pray for him." So we went over to where Sean was and she began to pray for Sean. Sean hadn't come alone. With him were two women, Angel and Michelle. As Harriet prayed, I felt the Lord put a scripture on my heart for Angel. So I told her that I had a word for her. I opened my Bible to Proverbs 31 and read verse 10 *"Who can find a virtuous woman? for her price is far above rubies."* I told her that verse and the following were for her. At that point, I had never seen her before and didn't know if I would ever see her again. There was nothing in particular that attracted me to her. She was short, a little overweight, had braces and short hair.

The next Saturday, Sean showed up again for the praise and worship time. He brought Michelle and Angel with him. This continued for months. Over the course of the next year, as this praise and worship ministry continued, we got to be pretty good friends. It turned out that Angel was a student at Christ for the Nations Institute in Dallas, and earned her living as a hairstylist. One Saturday morning only a few weeks after first meeting them, we had gone out to breakfast together again, and Sean wanted his hair styled. Angel didn't have a place to do it. My apartment was less than a mile from the Denny's where we were having breakfast, so I offered the use of my apartment.

That afternoon, my care group, a small home fellowship group from the church made up of singles, was to meet another singles care group in a park about a mile away from my apartment for a barbecue and volleyball game. I invited Sean and Angel to join us, which they did. When we got to the park, it looked like rain, but we started anyway. Between the two care groups over 40 people showed up. We managed to play most of one volleyball game before it started to rain. As it started to rain, everyone started trying to figure out what to do. God told me to invite them to my apartment. I said, "Lord, there are over 40 people here. How can they fit in my apartment?" The more I reasoned, the harder it rained. So I quickly volunteered my apartment and gave directions. Away we all went.

It was quite a crowd in that apartment. Finding a place was tough. We loaded the food on the dining room table. People were sitting everywhere. There were people in every room, people on the porch, people in the entry way. I settled at the keyboards and began to play. That seemed to help bring some order. Pretty quickly the rain stopped and the sun came out.

For some reason I didn't understand, I found myself wondering about Angel. Where was she in all this? When I caught myself doing this, I asked myself "Why did I care anyway? There are lots of people here. She can take care of herself." I left it at that.

Over the course of about two years, Angel and I became close friends. However, it was not a romantic relationship in any way. At one point, Angel went to Idaho, where she was from, for about three months. The Lord showed me that she would be coming back, which she did. All this time we were just friends. One day, I was at work, still working for Texas Instruments, at my Lewisville office. I was reading a technical article and felt the Holy Spirit interrupt me and tell me to call Angel. At that time, Angel was working as a secretary for Church on the Rock North America in the Church on the Rock offices. I knew the church phone number, so I called it and asked for Angel. We had a real nothin' conversation that didn't last five minutes. After I hung up, I thought to myself "That was odd" and went back to my business, proceeding to forget about it totally. After lunch that day, I had a meeting in another part of the building that took me away from my office for a few hours. When I returned, there was a message to "Call Angel". So I called Angel.

She said to me, "This morning, when you called me, the Lord told you to call, didn't He?"

I said, "Well, actually, yes He did".

"I have a confession to make", Angel said.

Uh oh, I thought, every woman that ever told me they had a confession to make told me something I didn't want to hear, and I would have to pray it "off" of me. "Yeah, well?" I said slowly.

"I have a confession to make." She repeated. "This morning when the Lord told you to call me, I asked Him to have you call me."

45

"Okay?" I replied, expectantly.

"That's it", she said.

"Okay, well I have to get back to work."

Conversation ended, I hung up. Something had changed. All of a sudden I had no peace. I had no idea why. It was disturbing. I looked at the clock. It was after 4:30 PM. I thought, "Good, I can go home soon and pray until I get some peace". I left as early as I could and drove home. I still had no peace. I started to pray, fervently. I didn't pray about the telephone conversation. I just started to pray the Lord's prayer as I usually did. Eventually, I got around to praying for my friends. I prayed for my friends Mike and Gerard. I prayed for Angel. One of the things I knew about Angel is that she wanted to get married. As I prayed for her, I asked the Lord to give her a godly man to be her husband. The Lord spoke to me, in as clear a voice as I ever heard, and said "You're him." Being the good charismatic Christian that I was, I stood up, and with everything in me, I said loudly "I bind you devil, in the name of Jesus!" When I did, I was hit with the overwhelming peace of God. That peace made me know, for sure, that it was really God speaking to me. However, I said to God, "Okay God, if this is *really* you, she is going to tell me, and I am going to forget about this completely until she does."

I was true to my word. I really did put this out of my mind, completely. I didn't even think about it or consider it. The following Thursday, at most a week from then, I got a phone call from some guy wanting me to look at some real estate for sale in a lakeside vacation community about two and one half hours drive away. I didn't want to go, but while I was on the phone, I felt the Lord told me to go. So I made an appointment for Saturday. When I got off the phone, I said to the Lord "Lord, I don't want to buy any property. What do you want me to go there for? I sure don't want to go alone. Maybe I'll ask Gerard to see if he will go with me." The Lord said, "Take Angel".

Angel and I, and a number of others had planned to meet the next evening, Friday night, to see a Cornerstone Theater play. This was a Christian drama group that generally had excellent productions. So I thought, Angel is supposed to be at that play tomorrow night. I'll ask her if she wants to go then. If God is really in it, it will work out.

Friday night came and we went to the show. I ended up sitting next to Angel. She told me that she and her friend Betty were going to go to Texarkana on Saturday and they were pretty excited about it. I said, "Well, I was going to ask you if you would go with me to look at some property tomorrow at Lake something or other (actually, I gave her the name of the lake, but I've long since forgotten it), but if you are going to Texarkana and can't go, I'll ask Gerard if he'll go with me." Angel replied, "I can go. We're not going to Texarkana until the evening." So we made plans to go together the next day.

The next day, I picked her up at her apartment and we went to see this property. The drive was two and a half hours there, about two hours looking at property I didn't buy, and two and a half hours back. We talked the whole way. Angel looked cute. She had lost weight, grown her hair out, and no longer wore braces. I couldn't help noticing. On the way back, I stopped by my apartment for some reason, before taking Angel home.

After we left my apartment, I said to Angel, "I know that God has called you to the ministry, but what is it He has called you to do?"

"I plead the fifth", she replied.

"Oh come on," I said, my curiosity really taking over, "What are you called to do?" Are you called to minister to tall people, short people, fat people, skinny people, black people, white people..." I kept going on, trying to get an answer. The drive from my apartment to hers was about 15 minutes. This kept up the entire way. She stonewalled me the entire trip.

Finally, as I was turning into the parking space in front of her apartment, I said, "Well, are you going to tell me what you are called to do or not?"

"Actually," she replied, "I've been praying about whether or not I'm called to be your wife."

"I'm not," I answered, "I'm having too much fun just being your friend." All the while I said this, I'm thinking, "I'm not praying about it, I already know."

"Well, if this is God, we'll have to do it you know." she said as she closed the door and walked off.

As I backed out of the parking space and drove off, I said to God, "God, what did you have to go and do that for? Now I have to do something about it."

The next day was Sunday. Angel was in Texarkana. I pondered what I would do. I decided that I would send her a bouquet of flowers at her office. Monday evening, after work, I phoned in my order to the florist. Then it hit me what I had done. Was I really ready for this? There was a wall in my life that I had just violated. I needed heart surgery. I cried out to God, and He took care of it. I was ready to go forward.

The next Sunday evening was our care group meeting. Angel had joined our care group and we had gone together. Afterwards, we went to the local Braums Ice Cream and fast food place, which was right next to the church, for a milk shake or burger or something. I had parked next door in the church parking lot. When we left and got into the car, I gave Angel our itinerary for the next few months. Among other things, I told her we would drive to Florida, meet my mother, pick up my sons and bring them back to stay for four to six weeks during the summer. I told her that my mother and her husband Grover could take them back to Florida with them.

Finally, I said "I guess I've done everything except ask you to marry me. Are you ready for that?"

"Yes," she said, "I do". (She later told me she said "I do" to try and add some romance to the moment.)

We then kissed for the very first time. We had never dated. We were friends, good friends. Now we were engaged. Just over three months later we were married. During those three months, we spent every possible minute together. We traveled to Idaho and met her parents over Memorial Day weekend, drove to Florida and back to meet my mother and pick up my sons over the Fourth of July weekend. Everything for our wedding was arranged. I had only three requirements for our wedding. First, I wanted it to be in my home church, my Father's house. Secondly, I wanted Bob Mason, the music pastor at our church to marry us. Finally, I wanted a couple of my close friends to be able to be there. Everything else was up to Angel.

The wedding came. Pastor Bob preached a message from Proverbs 31, verses 10 and following *"Who can find a virtuous woman? for her price is far above rubies."* I was amazed. Afterwards we went up to Pastor Bob and I told him, "Pastor Bob, you don't know what you did! The message you preached from Proverbs 31 was the exact word I gave Angel the day that we met."

Pastor Bob replied, "But you don't know what I know. I wasn't going to preach on this, but when I got up to speak, the Lord told me to preach on Proverbs 31. It seems that God has shown you that He set this up from the very beginning."

God is truly awesome! This amazing story is true. Every time I tell it, I'm still amazed. God's ways work! They often seem hard at the time, but ultimately His ways are always the best. As I write this today, I've been happily married for almost 16 years now. I have a wonderful wife and four more children.

Let's side track a bit on this issue of marriage and dating, or lack thereof. (If you are already married, submit your marriage to God and stay faithful.) In any case, let's see what the Word of God has to say about this. For a long time, I was convinced I should not date, that God would bring me my wife. This turned out to be true. Scripturally, however, I struggled with a basis for my stand. I was aware of Proverbs 18:22, which states *"Whoso findeth a wife findeth a good thing, and obtaineth favour of the LORD."* "Finding" a wife, seems to imply "seeking" a wife. However, 1 Corinthians 7:27 says to seek not a wife *"Art thou loosed from a wife? seek not a wife."* Both of these things couldn't be correct, could they? I am convinced that the Bible does not contradict itself, so I must be interpreting something incorrectly. Looking these up in the Hebrew and Greek respectively provided the answer. The word "find" or "findeth" (in King James English) in the Hebrew actually means "come forth". It is not that the word "find" is a wrong definition, but a better translation of this scripture is "He who has a wife come forth, has had a good thing come forth, and obtains the favor of the Lord". This does not imply seeking.

So, is seeking a wife wrong? I don't want to put a set of rules on you. You have to decide for yourself. Let's allow the scripture to speak. Genesis 6:2 states *"That the sons of God saw the daughters of men that they were fair; and they took them wives of all which **they** chose."* (emphasis added). As part of the same general thought, verse 6 of that same chapter states *"And it repented the LORD that he had made man on the earth, and it grieved him at his heart."* Obviously, there was much wickedness that grieved God, but verse 2 was lumped together with the other items that grieved God. Otherwise, it would not even make any sense in scripture to be there. Remember, we showed earlier those who are *"led by the Spirit of God are sons of God"* (Romans 8:14). The implication is that the "daughters of men" were not those led by the Spirit of God. This is implying an "unequal yoke". 2 Corinthians 6:14 states *"Be ye not unequally yoked together with unbelievers"* We know from King Solomon's example, that his unbelieving wives led him away from serving God with his whole heart. Since the "sons of God" did what they wanted, and not what God wanted, they became rebellious to God. I can understand why this grieves God.

What does this mean? It means that dating, the way the world does it, is the world's way, not God's way. For example, throughout the book of Song of Solomon it is continually stated (Example Song of Solomon 8:4) *"Daughters of Jerusalem, I charge you: Do not arouse or awaken love until it so desires."* (NIV) The King James version interprets the words "it so desires as "until he pleases". Other similar scriptures state this as "until it pleases". Pleases whom? Obviously we know this is not the flesh! It has to please God and your spirit. We all know that a kiss can change your entire relationship.

God shows us an example of how He will provide for a wife in Genesis 24. It is too long to put the entire story here, but it is very simple. Abraham did not want an unequally yoked wife for his son. He sent his servant to his relatives at Nahor to get a wife for him. Unless God ordained and set up this wife, it would not happen. She was going to have to make a commitment to marry someone that she had not even met, or ever seen. The servant realized this when he asked Abraham in verse 5 *"And the servant said unto*

51

him, Peradventure the woman will not be willing to follow me unto this land: must I needs bring thy son again unto the land from whence thou camest?" Abraham's response was (verses 6-8) *"Beware thou that thou bring not my son thither again. The LORD God of heaven, which took me from my father's house, and from the land of my kindred, and which spake unto me, and that sware unto me, saying, Unto thy seed will I give this land; he shall send his angel before thee, and thou shalt take a wife unto my son from thence. And if the woman will not be willing to follow thee, then thou shalt be clear from this my oath: only bring not my son thither again."* This was going to be a big step of faith. Abraham, Isaac, Rebekah, and the servant all had to be led by the Spirit of God to make this happen. As we know, it did in fact happen. When Rebekah was asked to go with the servant, she replied (verse 58) *"I will go".* She received Isaac as her husband by faith (verse 65) *"For she had said unto the servant, What man is this that walketh in the field to meet us? And the servant had said, It is my master: therefore she took a vail, and covered herself."* Isaac too, received Rebekah by faith (verse 67) *"And Isaac brought her into his mother Sarah's tent, and took Rebekah, and she became his wife; and he loved her"* All indications in the Bible are that this was a good marriage. It was definitely God's plan.

Are you single and want to be married? What do you do? First, Matthew 6:33 *"But seek ye first the kingdom of God, and his righteousness; and all these things shall be added unto you."* Second, Psalm 37:4 *"Delight thyself also in the LORD; and he shall give thee the desires of thine heart."* Ask God, and ask specifically (remember my testimony of the list). Matthew 7:7 and 8: *"Ask, and it shall be given you; seek, and ye shall find; knock, and it shall be opened unto you: For every one that asketh receiveth; and he that seeketh findeth; and to him that knocketh it shall be opened."* Practically, don't expect to stay home in your closet and have Mr. or Miss DreamBoat just show up out of the blue. Hebrews 10:25 *"Not forsaking the assembling of ourselves together, as the manner of some is"* and let me add, with members of the opposite sex. Apply this to your social life. Assemble together with single Christians that are equally yoked. Finally, be faithful where God puts you to serve, for this is your place of blessing. These principles apply in everything we do in our lives for *"God is faithful"* (1 Corinthians 1:9).

So, we can see that God's way's are not our ways and in the example above, they are not even remotely similar! One of the keys to knowing God as the Lord our Sanctification and God's ways is to know His word. This is something we should grow in every day of our life. Jesus said in John 17:17 *"Sanctify them through thy truth: thy word is truth."* Aside from prayer, reading the Bible is critical. For *"Man shall not live by bread alone, but by every word of God."* (Luke 4:4) We live by the word of God. Our minds are cleansed by the word. Ephesians 5:26 states *"That he might sanctify and cleanse it with the washing of water by the word"* Our promised land awaits, the kingdom of God!

Questions for consideration or discussion
1. What does "be holy for I am holy" mean to you? How do you apply this in your life?
2. Do people outside the church consider you "religious"? Is this because you live a true holy and sanctified life or is it because you live by a set of rules of "holiness"? Explain.
3. Give a personal testimony of how God has separated you from the things of the world. If you can't, what will you change?

4. Are you holding on to things of the world? What do you need to release to God?

5. Have you considered that you can know God's ways and thoughts? Or do God's ways seem mysterious to you? Explain.

6. Explain, in your own way, how God's ways and thoughts are different from your own. Why are they better ways? Better thoughts?

7. What important decisions or desires are there in your life where you really need to know God's ways and to apply them to your own ways?

Chapter 6
Beyond Understanding
The Lord our Peace

For ye shall go out with joy, and be led forth with peace (Isaiah 55:12}

In the last chapter, I spoke of not having peace, and also of "the overwhelming peace of God." It is obvious that I'm not referring to "peace" in the same manner that it is most often used. It is not the "absence of strife" or the "absence of war" that I am referring to. Rather, I am referring to an inner peace that is hard to describe if you've never experienced it. Jesus said *"Peace I leave with you, my peace I give unto you: not as the world giveth, give I unto you."* (John 14:27) It is a peace that you cannot experience without Jesus. It is not the peace that the world gives.

I have been told that in the former Soviet Union, there were many references to "peace". Apparently, this was something that was prevalent in the propaganda of the government. The civil unrest and crime in the United States and the western world were given as examples of why the communist system was better than the ways of the West. The only kind of peace in the former Soviet Union, was one of controlled peace. It was a false peace for *"there is no peace, saith the LORD, unto the wicked"* (Isaiah 48:22). Jesus distinctly separated this type of peace from that which is the peace of God. In John 16:33, Jesus said *"These things I have spoken unto you, that in me ye might have peace. In the world ye shall have tribulation: but be of good cheer; I have overcome the world."* The troubles of this world (tribulation) are separated from the peace of God. Our peace must be in Him for *"the chastisement of our peace was upon him"* (Isaiah 53:5).

55

God's peace is truly unique. I remember the first time I truly experienced it. I did not even realize it was from God at the time. Looking back though, I remember it so clearly. It made a major impression on me, even though I did not understand it. Philippians 4:7 states *"And the peace of God, which passeth all understanding, shall keep your hearts and minds through Christ Jesus"* It was back around 1983, in the midst of my rough years of separation which ultimately led to divorce. I had done everything that I could do to attempt to restore my failed marriage, but had realized that a divorce would happen no matter what I did. I was walking outside among the big trees in Washington State and dealing with this issue. I was "sort of" talking to God and to myself. I guess I was praying, but I didn't really consider it so. I wasn't asking for anything, just dealing with the reality of the situation that was totally out of my control. Suddenly, I had peace. I knew it would be okay. I didn't have any answers. I didn't have any direction. It was just okay. My marriage was over and I not only accepted that fact, but it was okay. In my natural mind, it made no sense. But somehow, I could let it go.

Over five years later, after I had proposed to Angel, we went and shopped for an engagement ring. Through my job at Texas Instruments, I was able to purchase diamond rings through a wholesaler, rather than a retailer. We made an appointment where Angel picked out a stone, and a setting for her engagement and wedding ring set. It would take the jeweler about a week to have the rings ready. I wanted to take her to dinner at a nice place to make the presentation of the engagement ring something special. I asked Angel where she wanted to go for dinner. Her first response was that she didn't know. I told her to think about it and let me know what she decided.

About a day or so later, she called me and told me that she wanted to go to "The Mansion at Turtle Creek". Apparently this was a place that many of her coworkers suggested as a top restaurant. She really didn't know much about it. I didn't either. However, after she told me this, there was unrest in me about the place every time I thought about it. I could not bring myself to make a reservation. I really didn't know why. I wasn't too concerned about it, since I assumed that just a few hours notice would be plenty. I just was not ready to make the reservation.

A few days later, the ring was ready and I went to the wholesaler to pick it up. While I was there, the jeweler asked me what my plan was for giving her the ring. I told him I would take her out to dinner at a nice restaurant and give it to her there. He asked me what restaurant we were planning. I told him that Angel had asked to go to The Mansion at Turtle Creek. He told me that it was a nice place but very expensive. I said something to him similar to "How expensive can it be? It's just a restaurant." He told me that it would "easily be over one hundred dollars per person. Even the forks are ALA-carte. If you want wine with dinner, it will be even more." This took me by surprise. I had never even heard of a restaurant so expensive! This was way over my budget. I could not do this.

As I drove away, I made a decision to tell Angel that we couldn't go to The Mansion. I would suggest a local Steak and Ale restaurant instead. As soon as I made this decision, I had the peace of God. I realized why I could not make the reservation at The Mansion. It was not God's will for me, nor was it a wise choice financially. Fortunately, Angel didn't mind at all. She was perfectly happy with Steak and Ale. She told me that she really didn't know anything about how to choose a restaurant. She had only picked

The Mansion based on recommendations from coworkers. The peace of God truly led me forth.

Over the years I have come to know where my peace comes from. I also have come to recognize when I don't have it. The peace of God that once was something I did not even know about is something that I won't live without. There are times that this peace is overwhelming. It goes beyond anything in the natural.

In my early days of learning to pray, God was dealing with all kinds of issues in my life. I would often find myself very frustrated, mostly with myself, because of what I considered a lack of progress in some matter I deemed important. Most of the times, this was because something was happening that I did not understand, or not happening when I thought it should. It was particularly frustrating to me when things did not seem to line up with what I believed God to be speaking to me. At one point, I became so frustrated with this that I actually was in the car yelling at God very loudly. In this world, when we lose our cool, and yell loudly at someone, they generally end up yelling back, and we end up in an argument. Fortunately, God is not like that. He did not yell at me. He did not even rebuke me, although I'm sure I deserved it. He didn't go away from me. He just gave me a peace that passes understanding. My anger left. My yelling subsided, and I immediately repented for yelling at God. I'm happy to say I don't do that anymore. I now understand that *"all things work together for good to them that love God, to them who are the called according to his purpose"* (Romans 8:28). Even now, I look back at yelling at God as really foolish. However, I have also learned that there is a transparency or intimacy with God that comes from pouring out your heart to God, even if it is something so obviously wrong as yelling at God. God loves us and understands us anyway. So we may as well be honest with Him.

Sometimes it is just amazing how God not only gives us peace in what can be trying situations, but how he works those situations out if we will just be sensitive to Him. I used to travel for business from the Dallas/Fort Worth area to Colorado Springs every month. About once every three months, this trip would also require me to travel to Ridgecrest, California. One of these trips, I arranged it over a weekend so that I would be in Colorado Springs one week, and Ridgecrest the next. Over the weekend, I planned to go to Phoenix to visit my sister. This worked out well since doing this actually saved the company money. As I left Colorado Springs for Phoenix, via Denver, on Friday night, the plane was late leaving. The connection out of Denver was the last scheduled flight of the night going that way. It looked like it would be close.

The flight from Colorado Springs to Denver was on a small twin-engine prop plane and it landed at a remote terminal area at the far end of the airport. I was just one of a number of passengers trying to make the connection. We ran to the gate for the connecting flight only to have just missed it. This was a bit distressing. So, after checking with the airline and getting rescheduled to an early morning flight, we were given lodging at the Denver Stapleton Inn, very close to the airport. I asked about my luggage. The attendant told me it had been rerouted to Phoenix via Las Vegas, and would arrive in Phoenix around 3 or 4 AM.

The problem was, I was in Denver, and my flight to Phoenix didn't even leave until around 7 AM. I wasn't happy about it, but I had peace. God also gave me an idea. I decided to go down to baggage claim and discuss my situation with the airline baggage service. It was late and very few people were around. The man at the baggage service quickly confirmed that my luggage was in fact rerouted to Phoenix via Las Vegas. I said to him, "Surely, it's not on the plane yet. It's probably in your baggage handling area." He agreed that I was probably right. I described my bag to him and asked if he would go and see if he could locate it. He told me that wasn't very likely. Also, he could not leave his service desk without someone to cover for him. I pointed out that there were very few people around, and that I could easily cover the desk for him, while he looked. Somewhat reluctantly, he agreed to go look.

About five minutes later he returned with my luggage in hand! I thanked him and headed off to catch the shuttle bus to the Stapleton Inn. In the morning, as I came to the airport with my fellow stranded travelers, I was completely refreshed. The rest of the passengers had to wear yesterday's clothes and, at best, had the complimentary toiletries provided by the hotel to clean up with. They all looked pretty haggard. I was the only one with any luggage, and the only one with clean clothes. It wasn't the best situation, but God not only gave me peace in it, he made it much better than it could have been.

I have experienced the peace of God in many situations. I've had peace when I've been told I would be laid off of a job in the midst of a recession. I've had peace guiding me in many major decisions. In fact, I won't make major decisions without the peace of God (and hopefully not even minor ones). I've had peace on business travel overseas where my plane flight was canceled and I had to reroute to a different city and take a bus to my final destination, not knowing if the party who was supposed to meet me would still be there when I arrived over eight hours late. I've had peace when an airline I had tickets on went on strike while I was overseas, and other similar travel situations. More recently, I've had a major peace in the midst of a trying situation on my job in the Telecom industry where thousands have been laid off around me. I've had peace during the tragedies of the terrorist attacks of September 11, 2001, and all the alerts following that event. The peace that I have in this is God's peace. It includes a "knowing" that it will be okay, regardless of what happens, for *"we know that all things work together for good to them that love God, to them who are the called according to his purpose"* (Romans 8:28). There is not enough space to even begin to list all the times in my life over the last 20 years that God's peace has intervened in my life. The peace of God has become a normal, but supernatural, part of my life.

So how can you experience God's peace in your life like I have? The Bible gives us a clear answer. Philippians 4:6 and 7 state *"Be careful* (anxious) *for nothing; but in every thing by prayer and supplication with thanksgiving let your requests be made known unto God. And the peace of God, which passeth all understanding, shall keep your hearts and minds through Christ Jesus."* Prayer and supplication will bring us this peace. .

Transparency with God in prayer will bring true peace. As we share our burdens, our trials, our fears, our hopes, our dreams and our disappointments with God, He pours out His peace in our hearts. We will then be able to *"let the peace of God rule in your hearts"* (Colossians 3:15). As you experience this peace, and let it be a guide to you, you are well on your way to your promised land, the kingdom of God.

Questions for consideration or discussion
1. Can you say honestly that you regularly experience the peace of God that passes all understanding? Give examples.

2. Can you give testimonies of specific times when this peace impacted your life, or helped you to make clear decisions? Expound on this.

3. What does it mean to you to be transparent with God?

4. If intimacy with God brings peace, how do you personally be intimate with God?

Chapter 7
Closer Than a Brother
The Lord Who is Present

Times of refreshing shall come from the presence of the Lord (Acts 3:19)

It is one thing to know in your mind that God is omnipresent. However, it is another thing altogether for that presence to become a constant part of your life. My desire is to live, act and fellowship with the Holy Spirit continuously. We are called to fellowship with Jesus. 1 Corinthians 1:9 states *"Ye were called unto the fellowship of his Son Jesus Christ our Lord."* The Greek word for this type of fellowship is "koinonia". This means to share, have a close partnership or communion. It is much closer than just that of casual acquaintance. God is looking for those who will walk with God. *"And Enoch walked with God after he begat Methuselah three hundred years"* (Genesis 5:22). This was not something that happened overnight for me. I am still learning to walk with God. However, the presence and fellowship of the Holy Spirit has become a constant part of my life.

There were times in my life where God seemed to be distant, even though I knew in my mind that He was there. Once, shortly after I had begun to pray regularly, things seemed to be rather hard. A number of things were not going well at all. One of these was a friend of mine, named Kevin, who was having major allergic reactions to something. He was spending more time in the hospital than anywhere else. There were other things that I was struggling with at the time also. I had been praying about these things for days, maybe even weeks, without ever seeming to get a breakthrough. One day, as I was praying, and rather frustrated, I said to God "Where are you when I need you?" I wasn't really expecting an answer, but God gave me one. He said to me "I'm right here." Needless to say, I felt pretty foolish. I knew that, but yet I guess I really didn't *know* it. God's word says *"I am with you always, even unto the end of the world"* (Matthew 28:20).

Before I began to pray the Lord's Prayer as an outline, not only did I not know how to pray, but I found any attempt at lengthy prayer boring. As I stated earlier, when I began to pray the Lord's Prayer as an outline, I had an *experience* with God. I began to experience His presence. This is what brings me to the place of prayer every day. Every day is not necessarily a glorious time in His presence, but every day He meets me in the place of prayer. This is what fills my life and what brings me back every time. This becomes a time of intimacy. I find there are days when I'm very fervent in prayer. Other days, it seems hard. However, one thing is consistent. If I can focus on God, and hallow His name, I will know His presence during that time. Even when I'm drowsy, or sometimes distracted, I generally manage to have time with Him. It is a precious time, and it brings me back daily. From this I am able to begin to abide with God. 1 Corinthians 7:24 states *"Brethren, let every man, wherein he is called, therein abide with God."*

This is the place that I find few Christians experience. It is the most holy place. In the old testament, only the high priest could enter the most holy place, behind the second veil of the temple, *"And after the second veil, the tabernacle which is called the Holiest of all"* (Hebrews 9:3). Also, the high priest could only enter this place once a year on the Day of Atonement. *"But into the second* (veil) *went the high priest alone once every year, not without blood, which he offered for himself, and for the errors of the people: The Holy Ghost this signifying, that the way into the holiest of all was not yet made manifest, while as the first tabernacle was yet standing"* (Hebrews 9: 7-8). The Bible states that when Jesus was crucified, *"the veil of the temple was rent in twain from the top to the bottom"* (Mark 15:38, see also Matthew 27:51 and Luke 23:45). This is showing us that Jesus made a way into the most holy place through His blood. We are to have *"boldness to enter into the holiest by the blood of Jesus"* (Hebrews 10:19) Jesus said that he did not come to put aside the old covenant, but rather to fulfill it. Jesus said *"Think not that I am come to destroy the law, or the prophets: I am not come to destroy, but to fulfil"* (Matthew 5:17). It is the blood of Jesus that has purchased for us the covenant promises ("covenant names" of God) of the Old Testament (the law).

The most holy place today is not in some man-made temple. 1 Corinthians 3:16 states *"Know ye not that ye are the temple of God, and that the Spirit of God dwelleth in you?"*. Today, the presence of God in the most holy place is something that we can experience daily through the blood of Jesus. This is what I experienced, really for the first time, as I began to pray the Lord's Prayer as an outline. This is what draws me back to the place of prayer daily. As it was in the Old Testament, the most holy place is a place where there is a manifestation of the presence of God. It is something that we *know* is real. It is His presence in this place that truly changes our lives.

The Bible shows us that there is another way to enter the presence of God. Psalms 100:4 states *"Enter into his gates with thanksgiving, and into his courts with praise"* and *"come before his presence with singing"* (Psalm 100:2). We know that *"then went king David in, and sat before the LORD"* (2 Samuel 7:18). He went and sat right before the Ark of the Covenant, where the presence of God was. He did this without blood sacrifices. He did it when it was not the Day of

Atonement. He was not even of the tribe of Levi, much less a Levitical priest, yet he had access to God's presence. How did David do this? He was one who praised and worshipped the Lord with all his might. 2 Samuel 6:14 says *"David danced before the LORD with all his might"*.

Virtually every Christian church service that I've ever been in, regardless of denomination, has some type of what is called a praise and worship time. However, many of these are nothing more than "song services". Many times, even the songs are not sung with any heart, by a large proportion of the congregation. Some people don't participate in the singing at all. This is far from the example David gave of *"all his might"*. Jesus said (John 4:23-24) *"But the hour cometh, and now is, when the true worshippers shall worship the Father in spirit and in truth: for the Father seeketh such to worship him. God is a Spirit: and they that worship him must worship him in spirit and in truth."* Worshipping in spirit is to worship him with our inner most being. Worshipping in truth is to worship without pretense. To do this requires giving our entire spirit, soul, and body into worship. If we do something in praise and worship to be seen by man, we do it with pretense. Conversely, if we don't do something in praise and worship because we are concerned about what others think, is to not give our all to God. We then allow our pride to get in the way, and we are not worshipping in spirit. This can include simple things like singing with all of our heart, raising our hands, or stepping out to praise the Lord in the dance as David did. Praise and worship is not about singing. It is also not about dancing, raising hands, clapping hands or any similar outward expression. These are all things we may or may not do when we praise and worship. However, they are not what praise and worship is about. Praise and worship is about giving our all before God, regardless of what others may think.

There is a man I've been praying for and witnessing to for many years, who has yet to receive Jesus as savior and Lord. During one of our many conversations on this subject, he stated something to the effect of "I just can't understand a God who would want to be worshipped." In his mind, worship is a degrading experience. However, true worship is a time in God's presence like none other. We give our worship to God and receive from Him at the same time. It is an intimate and powerful time. When I was doing the Saturday morning praise and worship sessions there were times that the presence of God was so strong I could barely continue. I would often worship at the piano and play with my eyes closed. Sometimes I would not open them for over an hour. During these times I was always amazed that I could continue to play the piano at all. I was not amazed that I could play with my eyes closed, but I was amazed that I was not overcome by the powerful presence of an awesome God that I felt. God's presence was so "thick" you could almost touch it. This is something that is hard to describe. It is a place I long to be always. It is a place that we can all experience as we give ourselves in praise and worship.

The Bible gives us an example of this awesome presence of God. 2 Chronicles 5:13 and 14 state *"It came even to pass, as the trumpeters and singers were as one, to make one sound to be heard in praising and thanking the LORD; and when they lifted up their voice with the trumpets and cymbals and instruments of musick, and praised the LORD, saying, For he is good; for his mercy endureth for ever: that then the house was filled with a cloud, even the house of the LORD; So that the priests could not stand to minister by reason of the cloud: for the glory of the LORD had filled the house of God."* This presence of God is accessible to us today.

It was during a church praise and worship service that I was baptized in the Holy Spirit. The church I attended was a charismatic or "spirit-filled" church. The praise and worship was extremely participatory and included singing, clapping hands, raising hands, and some would even dance. The congregation believed in and experienced speaking in tongues. I knew that speaking in tongues was in the Bible, but I sure did not understand it at all. During one of the weekday evening services that I attended, the preacher called for those who did not speak in tongues to come forward and be prayed for to receive the Holy Spirit. I did not speak in tongues. I also didn't understand what tongues had to do with being baptized with the Holy Spirit. I thought I already had the Holy Spirit. Although I wasn't really sure of what I thought about this, I went forward along with about another dozen people.

I was surrounded by 10-15 men laying hands on me, praying for me, praying in tongues for me and telling me things like "let it loose" and "you can do it". To be honest, it was confusing. I wasn't real comfortable with all the hands on me, nor did I appreciate being expected to do something I had no clue about. I did not speak in tongues. They continued to pray for about ten minutes or so. After about 2 minutes, this "ordeal" became agonizingly long to me. I could not wait for this to be over. Finally, the preacher had mercy and moved us on to something else.

A week later, before the service started, the preacher said "Later on, for those of you who do not yet speak in tongues, we'll have a time of prayer where you can receive the Holy Spirit." I thought, "Oh no, not again." I prayed to God a prayer something like

"Oh God, I do not want to go through that again. If this praying in tongues stuff is from You and something You want me to have, I want it. If it's not, I don't. One thing I absolutely don't want to do is get prayed for like that again." The service started with praise and worship. As we moved from exuberant praise into worship, I was really reaching out to God with my heart. My hands were raised, my eyes were closed and I was singing the worship chorus with the congregation. Suddenly, I heard words come out of my mouth that didn't come from my brain. I started to sing in tongues. I immediately stopped since it surprised me. Then I found I could readily do it again, at will. Yet, it was not something I was doing in my brain. It was coming straight from my spirit to my mouth, and I was definitely glorifying God with tongues. As the service moved to the preaching, I realized I would not have to go forward with those who did not speak in tongues. What a relief! God had baptized me with the Holy Spirit during worship.

For a while, I really just thought that I had received the gift of tongues. In my understanding, I already had the Holy Spirit. The reality was that I did have a measure of the Holy Spirit. I was saved. However, I had not been baptized with the Holy Spirit, even though I thought I had. John the Baptist stated *"I indeed baptize you with water unto repentance: but he that cometh after me is mightier than I, whose shoes I am not worthy to bear: he shall baptize you with the Holy Ghost, and with fire"* (Matthew 3:11) Somehow, things became different in my life. I was much bolder as a witness. This lined up with Jesus' last words on the earth before being taken up into heaven (Acts 1:8) *"But ye shall receive power, after that the Holy Ghost is come upon you: and ye shall be witnesses unto me both in Jerusalem, and in all Judaea, and in Samaria, and unto the uttermost part of the earth."* I also seemed to have a much greater hunger for the word of God. Reading the Bible became more than just something I did. It became a passion that I would not live without.

Over a period of time, probably about a year, the Holy Spirit became more and more real to me. He was not just something that I talked about or referred to in distant terms. He was not just the third person of the Trinity. He became my companion, a real "person" that was always there. As I realized one day how much the Holy Spirit had become a "person" in my life, I found myself wanting even more knowledge of Him. I asked the Holy Spirit a really dumb question. I said "Holy Spirit, what is your name?" He answered me clearly, "Jesus". I felt silly. I knew that, but once again I guess I really didn't, or I wouldn't have asked the question. The Bible calls the Holy Spirit the "Spirit of Jesus". Acts 16:7 (NIV) *"When they came to the border of Mysia, they tried to enter Bithynia, but the Spirit of Jesus would not allow them to."* I had learned the meaning of the scripture *"there is a friend that sticketh closer than a brother."* (Proverbs 18:24)

Unfortunately, in many American churches, speaking in tongues not only doesn't exist, it has even been spoken against. This is contrary to God's word which states *"forbid not to speak with tongues"* (1 Corinthians 14:39). Some have gone so far as to call it as from the devil. I can assure you that it is not. However, you should not take my word for it. The written word of God must be your guide. Acts chapter 2 gives the account of Pentecost, where the baptism of the Holy Spirit happened first.

> *"And when the day of Pentecost was fully come, they were all with one accord in one place. And suddenly there came a sound from heaven as of a rushing mighty wind, and it filled all the*

house where they were sitting. And there appeared unto them cloven tongues like as of fire, and it sat upon each of them. And they were all filled with the Holy Ghost, and began to speak with other tongues, as the Spirit gave them utterance. And there were dwelling at Jerusalem Jews, devout men, out of every nation under heaven. Now when this was noised abroad, the multitude came together, and were confounded, because that every man heard them speak in his own language. And they were all amazed and marvelled, saying one to another, Behold, are not all these which speak Galilaeans? And how hear we every man in our own tongue, wherein we were born? Parthians, and Medes, and Elamites, and the dwellers in Mesopotamia, and in Judaea, and Cappadocia, in Pontus, and Asia, Phrygia, and Pamphylia, in Egypt, and in the parts of Libya about Cyrene, and strangers of Rome, Jews and proselytes, Cretes and Arabians, we do hear them speak in our tongues the wonderful works of God. And they were all amazed, and were in doubt, saying one to another, What meaneth this? Others mocking said, These men are full of new wine. But Peter, standing up with the eleven, lifted up his voice, and said unto them, Ye men of Judaea, and all ye that dwell at Jerusalem, be this known unto you, and hearken to my words: For these are not drunken, as ye suppose, seeing it is but the third hour of the day. But this is that which was spoken by the prophet Joel; And it shall come to pass in the last days, saith God, I will pour out of my Spirit upon all flesh: and your sons and your daughters shall prophesy, and your young men shall see visions, and your old men shall dream dreams:" (Acts 2:1-17)

This sets the standard for being filled with the Holy Spirit. The disciples, 120 of them (see Acts 1:15), spoke in tongues as the Spirit gave them utterance. Many, from other nations, heard Galileans speaking in their own native tongues. This shows that what they were speaking had intelligence to it. Others, mocking, thought they were drunk. This infers that all those present probably did not understand what was being spoken. Peter explained it as the fulfillment of the prophecy of Joel. Peter also stated *"Then Peter said unto them, Repent, and be baptized every one of you in the name of Jesus Christ for the remission of sins, and ye shall receive the gift of the Holy Ghost. For the promise is unto you, and to your children, and to all that are afar off, even as many as the Lord our God shall call."* (Acts 2:38 and 39) He clearly stated that the promise of the Holy Spirit, as just seen, was not just for them, but for all generations (afar off).

The next time the Bible documents people being filled with the Holy Spirit is in Acts chapter 8.

"But there was a certain man, called Simon, which beforetime in the same city used sorcery, and bewitched the people of Samaria, giving out that himself was some great one: To whom they all gave heed, from the least to the greatest, saying, This man is the great power of God. And to him they had

regard, because that of long time he had bewitched them with sorceries. But when they believed Philip preaching the things concerning the kingdom of God, and the name of Jesus Christ, they were baptized, both men and women. Then Simon himself believed also: and when he was baptized, he continued with Philip, and wondered, beholding the miracles and signs which were done. Now when the apostles which were at Jerusalem heard that Samaria had received the word of God, they sent unto them Peter and John: Who, when they were come down, prayed for them, that they might receive the Holy Ghost: (For as yet he was fallen upon none of them: only they were baptized in the name of the Lord Jesus.) Then laid they their hands on them, and they received the Holy Ghost. And when Simon saw that through laying on of the apostles' hands the Holy Ghost was given, he offered them money, Saying, Give me also this power, that on whomsoever I lay hands, he may receive the Holy Ghost." (Acts 8:9-19)

This passage does not directly state that they spoke with tongues. However, there is evidence that they did. Simon *saw* something. This passage also makes clear a few other points. First, that the people of Samaria were already saved and baptized, but had not yet received the baptism of the Holy Spirit. Second, that this group received the Holy Spirit through the laying on of hands.

The next record in the book of Acts of believers being baptized with the Holy Spirit is in Acts chapter 10.

> *"While Peter yet spake these words, the Holy Ghost fell on all them which heard the word. And they of the circumcision which believed were astonished, as many as came with Peter, because that on the Gentiles also was poured out the gift of the Holy Ghost. For they heard them speak with tongues, and magnify God. Then answered Peter, Can any man forbid water, that these should not be baptized, which have received the Holy Ghost as well as we?"* (Acts 10:44-47)

Once again, those baptized with the Holy Spirit spoke in tongues. It was separate from water baptism. The Holy Spirit was given, in this case, without anyone laying hands. The gift was given to Gentiles for the first time. Peter specifically stated that they had received the Holy Spirit the same as he and the others had. This he also restated in Acts 11:15 as he testified of this experience *"And as I began to speak, the Holy Ghost fell on them, as on us at the beginning"*

The next reference to the baptism of the Holy Spirit in the book of Acts is rather vague.

> *"And a certain Jew named Apollos, born at Alexandria, an eloquent man, and mighty in the scriptures, came to Ephesus. This man was instructed in the way of the Lord; and being fervent in the spirit, he spake and taught diligently the things of the Lord, knowing only the baptism of John. And he began to speak boldly in the synagogue: whom when Aquila and Priscilla had heard, they*

took him unto them, and expounded unto him the way of God more perfectly." (Acts 18:24-26}

In this case, we see that Apollos was bold and instructed in the ways of the Lord. However, he knew only the "baptism of John" (a reference that he did not know the baptism of the Holy Spirit). Aquila and Priscilla had to more adequately explain to him the way of God.

The next reference we see to the baptism of the Holy Spirit is in Acts 19.

"And it came to pass, that, while Apollos was at Corinth, Paul having passed through the upper coasts came to Ephesus: and finding certain disciples, He said unto them, Have ye received the Holy Ghost since ye believed? And they said unto him, We have not so much as heard whether there be any Holy Ghost. And he said unto them, Unto what then were ye baptized? And they said, Unto John's baptism. Then said Paul, John verily baptized with the baptism of repentance, saying unto the people, that they should believe on him which should come after him, that is, on Christ Jesus. When they heard this, they were baptized in the name of the Lord Jesus. And when Paul had laid his hands upon them, the Holy Ghost came on them; and they spake with tongues, and prophesied." (Acts 19:1-6)

In this passage we see once again, believers that had been baptized in water, but had not been baptized with the Holy Spirit. We see the baptism of the Holy Spirit given at the laying on of hands. In this case, Paul, who laid hands, was not one of the original 12 apostles. When the Holy Spirit came on them, they spoke with tongues. One of the arguments given against tongues and the baptism of the Holy Spirit is that it "was given only by the laying on of the apostles hands". As can be seen, Paul was an apostle, but not one of the original twelve. He did not receive the Holy Spirit at Pentecost. The inference in Acts 18:24-26 is that Apollos received the baptism of the Holy Spirit through Aquila and Priscilla. We also have Acts 8:9-19 where the Holy Spirit was given without anyone laying hands. This is clearly not a valid argument.

Another argument I have heard against tongues is that they should only be used when there is an interpreter. This argument is based on 1 Corinthians chapter 14.

Follow after charity, and desire spiritual gifts, but rather that ye may prophesy. For he that speaketh in an unknown tongue speaketh not unto men, but unto God: for no man understandeth him; howbeit in the spirit he speaketh mysteries. But he that prophesieth speaketh unto men to edification, and exhortation, and comfort. He that speaketh in an unknown tongue edifieth himself; but he that prophesieth edifieth the church. I would that ye all spake with tongues, but rather that ye prophesied: for greater is he that prophesieth than he that speaketh with tongues, except he interpret, that the church may receive edifying.

Now, brethren, if I come unto you speaking with tongues, what shall I profit you, except I shall speak to you either by revelation, or by knowledge, or by prophesying, or by doctrine? And even things without life giving sound, whether pipe or harp, except they give a distinction in the sounds, how shall it be known what is piped or harped? For if the trumpet give an uncertain sound, who shall prepare himself to the battle? So likewise ye, except ye utter by the tongue words easy to be understood, how shall it be known what is spoken? for ye shall speak into the air. There are, it may be, so many kinds of voices in the world, and none of them is without signification. Therefore if I know not the meaning of the voice, I shall be unto him that speaketh a barbarian, and he that speaketh shall be a barbarian unto me.

Even so ye, forasmuch as ye are zealous of spiritual gifts, seek that ye may excel to the edifying of the church. Wherefore let him that speaketh in an unknown tongue pray that he may interpret. For if I pray in an unknown tongue, my spirit prayeth, but my understanding is unfruitful.

What is it then? I will pray with the spirit, and I will pray with the understanding also: I will sing with the spirit, and I will sing with the understanding also. Else when thou shalt bless with the spirit, how shall he that occupieth the room of the unlearned say Amen at thy giving of thanks, seeing he understandeth not what thou sayest? For thou verily givest thanks well, but the other is not edified. I thank my God, I speak with tongues more than ye all: Yet **in the church** *I had rather speak five words with my understanding, that by my voice I might teach others also, than ten thousand words in an unknown tongue."* (1 Corinthians 14:1-19 emphasis added)

It is quite clear in this passage that Paul is speaking of orderly worship in the church. He clearly is not saying only to speak in tongues when an interpreter is present. This is confirmed in Jude 1:20 *"But ye, beloved, building up yourselves on your most holy faith, praying in the Holy Ghost"* and also in Romans 8:26 *"Likewise the Spirit also helpeth our infirmities: for we know not what we should pray for as we ought: but the Spirit itself maketh intercession for us with groanings which cannot be uttered".* Also, Paul even makes clear that singing with the spirit can also be orderly. His reference is specifically to that of giving a message in tongues. In that specific case, an interpreter should be present. This argument also does not stand up to scrutiny.

Every passage on this subject in the book of Acts either directly or indirectly indicates that being baptized with the Holy Spirit results in speaking in tongues. We have seen that it is distinct from salvation and water baptism. We have seen that the Holy Spirit can be given by the laying on of hands, or not. We have seen that it is for all generations, which means that it is for you and I today, for *"Jesus Christ the same yesterday, and today, and forever"* (Hebrews 13:8). We know that *"there is no respect of persons with God"* (Romans 2:11) so we do not need an apostle to receive the baptism of the Holy Spirit.

In the Gospel of John, Jesus spoke to us about the Holy Spirit. John 14:16-17 state *"And I will pray the Father, and he shall give you another Comforter, that he may abide with you for ever; Even the Spirit of truth; whom the world cannot receive, because it seeth him not, neither knoweth him: but ye know him; for he dwelleth with you, and shall be in you."* Here He separated the Holy Spirit as one that was with the disciples, but would later be *in* the disciples. John 14:26 states *"But the Comforter, which is the Holy Ghost, whom the Father will send in my name, he shall teach you all things, and bring all things to your remembrance, whatsoever I have said unto you."* John 15:26 later states *"But when the Comforter is come, whom I will send unto you from the Father, even the Spirit of truth, which proceedeth from the Father, he shall testify of me".* These passages tell us some of the functions of the Holy Spirit. In John 16:7, Jesus makes it clear that he must depart before the Holy Spirit is given. *"Nevertheless I tell you the truth; It is expedient for you that I go away: for if I go not away, the Comforter will not come unto you; but if I depart, I will send him unto you."*

Must you speak in tongues? Obviously you do not. The Bible is quite clear that you are saved by faith, not by speaking in tongues. However, do you want everything God has for you? Do you desire to take all of your promised land? You will need the power of the Holy Spirit to do it. How do you receive the Holy Spirit?

> *"And I say unto you, Ask, and it shall be given you; seek, and ye shall find; knock, and it shall be opened unto you. For every one that asketh receiveth; and he that seeketh findeth; and to him that knocketh it shall be opened. If a son shall ask bread of any of you that is a*

father, will he give him a stone? or if he ask a fish, will he for a fish give him a serpent? Or if he shall ask an egg, will he offer him a scorpion? If ye then, being evil, know how to give good gifts unto your children: how much more shall your heavenly Father give the Holy Spirit to them that ask him?" (Luke 11:9-13)

"I will never leave thee, nor forsake thee." (Hebrews 13:5)

Questions for consideration or discussion

1. Is the Holy Spirit a real person to you? Explain.

2. Is the presence of God a reality in your life? Can you give a testimony of God's presence and how He revealed Himself to you?

3. Do you experience God's presence when you pray? Do you have he reality of the Most Holy Place? Explain

4. What does praise and worship mean to you?

5. What does worshipping in spirit and in truth mean to you? How do you do this?

6. Do you experience God's presence in your church during praise and worship or is it just singing songs?

7. Do you speak in tongues? If not do you want to do so? Why or why not?

8. Do you think it is God's will for you to speak in tongues? Explain

9. What does being filled with the Holy Spirit mean to you?

10. What does the power of the Spirit mean to you?

Chapter 8
Nothing is Impossible with God
The Lord our Healer

"Therefore if any man be in Christ, he is a new creature: old things are passed away; behold, all things are become new." (2 Corinthians 5:17)

As I look at my life over the past 20 years, I am continually amazed at the wondrous love of God and what He has done for me. From my experience, most Christians don't really believe that God heals or, more accurately, that He will heal them. Yet God's promise to his people is that *"I am the LORD that healeth thee"* (Exodus 15:26). The Hebrew for this is "Jehovah-rophe". Jehovah, the Hebrew word for God, means "the eternal". Rophe means to heal thoroughly and make whole. So God is "the eternal who heals us thoroughly and makes us whole". This is a complete healing of spirit, soul, and body. He heals us *"yesterday, and today, and forever"* (Hebrews 13:8). I found out that I could apply this specifically. God was able to heal my "yesterday".

As I started my story in 1984, that I shared back in chapter one, I was what most would consider an over comer, and what the world would typically consider successful. At that time, I was a Lieutenant in the United States Navy nuclear power program. I was a qualified US Navy Surface Warfare Officer, and a qualified Chief Engineer for US Navy nuclear power plants. I had approximately 140 people working for me as Main Propulsion Assistant, Assistant Chief Engineer, and Ship's Test Officer during overhaul of a nuclear guided missile cruiser. I had done more, and had more responsibilities by age 25 than many people ever do in their entire lifetime. However, this did not ever satisfy me.

Most Christians would say that this was due to the void in my life caused by not serving God. I greatly agree that not serving God will leave a great void in your heart, but this was not the crux of the issue for me. As a young boy growing up, I was very insecure. Whenever I was under pressure about anything, I would generally end up failing.

For example, one of my favorite things as a young boy was to play baseball. In neighborhood pickup games I was as good a player as most of the neighbors. However, in the organized local intramural leagues (a "Boy's Club" similar to little league), I generally played rather poorly. As a hitter, I would mostly strike out or walk. As a fielder, I did well unless the ball was hit straight at me. If I had time to think about it, I would find ways to mess it up. At one point I wanted to be a pitcher. I worked very hard at becoming a pitcher. I threw hundreds of balls a day at a target. I could hit it consistently. I could do the same throwing to a catcher. For my age, I had quite the sinking fast ball. The problem was, as soon as a hitter stepped in, I became wild, and because of my speed, I was dangerously wild. My insecurity would not let me succeed. I was trapped by it.

As I grew older, I learned to overcome this insecurity. I even became a reasonable baseball player under pressure. I did not let anything stop me. If someone said I could not do something I thought I wanted to do, I was determined to show them that they were wrong. I did whatever it took to succeed. One thing I'm happy to say I didn't do is to use others to get what I wanted. When I first married at age 19, a few people said I was ruining my life, that I would never finish college and other similar "you can't do that" statements. I was determined to show them wrong. I did finish college and go on to be an officer in the US Navy. I became a nuclear engineer. This is

82

supposed to be the top 1% of the top 1% of the Navy. I determined to even excel at that. As I took over as Main Propulsion Assistant, which is normally a senior Lieutenant or even Junior Lieutenant Commander's job, I was only a frocked Lieutenant. This means that I wore the bars, but was still only receiving the pay of Lieutenant Junior Grade, and my date of rank as a Lieutenant was in the future.

As I left the Navy and took on a new challenge at Texas Instruments, this pattern continued. I was successful in establishing an entire new "design for manufacturing" engineering group, something numerous others before me had apparently failed at. By this time, I was serving God with all my heart, and His hand was definitely in my success. However, inside of me, something was not satisfied.

For a period of around three years after I began to pray regularly, God let me see things in me, that were not like Him at all. He showed me things, that I've now long since forgotten, that caused me to react rather than to respond in situations. Sometimes I would be defensive. Sometimes I would become angry and verbally attack others. Each time that I saw something in me that was not like God, I would go to Him and ask Him to change me. Almost every time, God would show me some situation or person in my past, generally in my childhood, that had hurt me. In most of these cases, there were people I needed to forgive. As I forgave these people, and asked for God's healing, He would supernaturally change me, healing my past. Even though some of these things were big in my eyes, I had enough faith to see God as bigger. The situations where the devil had place in me had the light of the gospel shedding away the darkness. The hooks were removed, and I became free from them.

Eventually, I hit the "mother load". God showed me things from my past that seemed insurmountable to me. He showed me that I was still trying to please my father. Now understand that by this time, my father had been dead for 10 years. God showed me things from being a little child, probably three to four years old, where I didn't seem to measure up (at least in my own eyes, probably not my Dad's eyes). He showed me things that continued from that time up until shortly before my Dad died. One thing brought to my remembrance was particularly painful.

As I was completing high school, I was trying very hard to get a scholarship to college. One of the most promising routes in my eyes was a military scholarship. I applied for Army, Navy, and Air Force ROTC scholarships, plus I applied to the US Coast Guard Academy. My Dad, who had worked as a civilian for the US Navy Department for over 32 years, apparently had some connections. Notice, I did not say that I had applied to the US Naval Academy at Annapolis, Maryland. This was only 18 miles away from where I grew up, and I had been there a number of times. I did not want to go to school there. However, as I applied for these other scholarships, apparently all the things necessary to apply to the Naval Academy were completed except one. I needed an appointment to the Academy.

On night, I received a phone call from some US Navy Commander or Captain, I really don't remember, asking me if I wanted to go to the Naval Academy. He basically said, that he was in a position where he could virtually ensure me that I would get an appointment if I wanted one. He told me that he had already reviewed my application, physical, and other papers and I was a good candidate. I turned him down. I did not want to go to school there. I told him I did not even apply, so I wasn't even sure what he meant by having reviewed my application.

A few months later, I was awarded a full scholarship from the US Navy to go to college at any of approximately 50 universities nation wide that offered an NROTC program. (I had to apply and be accepted to the college I chose independently of course.) During college, I would receive full tuition, books, fees, and $100.00 per month from the Navy, and would have the same rank, midshipman, as those that went to the Naval Academy. Upon graduation, I would be commissioned in the regular Navy, as an Ensign. This was exactly the same as those who graduated from the Naval Academy.

Well, one day, I went with my Dad to Crystal City, Virginia, to the office where he used to work for the Navy Department. He introduced me to a US Navy Lt. Commander somebody or other. This was all okay except that when he introduced me, he didn't introduce me as just his son, nor did he introduce me as his son who had recently received a full scholarship from the Navy. Instead, he introduced me as his son who turned down an appointment to the Naval Academy. This hit hard. All my life, it seemed that no matter what I did, it was never good enough for my Dad. Here I now had a scholarship from the Navy that would ultimately make me a US Navy officer, something that my Dad held as one of his highest ideals, and he wasn't happy with me because I didn't want to go to the Naval Academy.

Along with all the other things in my life from a very young age, things I don't remember, but God knew about, I had buried this in my past. But God had brought it back to my memory. I had no trouble forgiving my Dad for this. I never once questioned that he loved me. I was absolutely sure that he did. I just didn't understand, and it had seriously and deeply hurt me. It looked huge to me. It seemed like a mountain I could not get past. I remember telling God, after He showed me all of this, that it seemed impossible to be free of this. It was so deeply ingrained in me. I could not even imagine being free of it. This is what drove my insecurity. I had overcome my insecurity, but I had never been healed of it. I was still in bondage to it. I was a driven man. I was not a free man.

Something in me just knew that I needed help. Obviously God was the one who had to free me. However, I needed help just to believe that He could or that He would. I went to my friend Harriet and told her I needed her to pray with me. At first she struggled to understand what the issue was, but she saw me in distress and took time to try to understand. After ten minutes or so of discussion, we prayed in agreement about this issue, that God would set me free. It turns out that this is a scriptural principle, although I didn't fully understand it at the time. *"Confess your faults one to another, and pray one for another, that ye may be healed"* (James 5:16).

A few more months went by. The times of calling out for God's healing abated. Something had changed. One morning, I looked in the mirror and saw myself differently. For the first time in my life, I looked in the mirror and liked the person I saw there. Up until that time, I didn't even know that I didn't like myself. Now, as I looked at myself, and liked who I saw, I realized that it was the first time. I was free, *really* free! Free like I had never been free before. I was no longer insecure. I was no longer a driven man. I was no longer driven to excel. I was free to excel. It was awesome. Life was better than I ever imagined it could be. God had healed my hurts and set me free! *Jesus said "Ye shall know the truth, and the truth shall make you free"* (John 8:32). The new creation God had made me was actually beginning to manifest in my life.

Unfortunately, this is not what I generally see in the church today. I see people who have often learned to overcome their faults and hurts, but they really aren't free from them. If you try to open the subject of the healing, freeing power of God, they'll virtually always tell you that they've "done that", they've "experienced that", they've "been set free". Then, most of the time they will tell you of some book they've read, or some class that they took, or some deliverance session that they've had and how they are free. I've never yet heard one talk about the awesome healing power of God and how He sets them free yesterday, today, and forever. I have never heard one yet be able to give testimony of the same.

It's not that these classes, books, or sessions aren't good. People probably really do get free from some things through them. I've been through some of these myself and I've yet to go through one that wasn't scripturally sound. The problem is that none of them can get you to the place, in and by themselves, that you really *know* God as the Lord your healer. You have to experience this for yourself. You also have to be able to appropriate God's healing for yourself regularly. The world we live in ensures that we all need healing regularly.

What is keeping Christians from not seeking the Lord our Healer and His healing? I personally believe that it is pride. We want to think that we "have already done that". This somehow makes us a "mature" Christian. This is a sure recipe for failure. *"Pride goeth before destruction, and an haughty spirit before a fall"* (Proverbs 16:18). Even though I have been free of "big things" from my past now for many years, I still have need of the Lord to heal me regularly. The fallen world that we live in will guarantee that there is always someone or something to offend or hurt you. Until we can fully grasp the healing of God daily, we risk being put back in bondage to a new hurt. *"If the Son therefore shall make you free, ye shall be free indeed"* (John 8:36)

Let us look at some scripture to support all of this.

"Then came Peter to him, and said, Lord, how oft shall my brother sin against me, and I forgive him? till seven times? Jesus saith unto him, I say not unto thee, Until seven times: but, Until seventy times seven. Therefore is the kingdom of heaven likened unto a certain king, which would take account of his servants. And when he had begun to reckon, one was brought unto him, which owed him ten thousand talents. But forasmuch as he had not to pay, his lord commanded him to be sold, and his wife, and children, and all that he had, and payment to be made. The servant therefore fell down, and worshipped him, saying, Lord, have patience with me, and I will pay thee all. Then the lord of that servant was moved with compassion, and loosed him, and forgave him the debt. But the same servant went out, and found one of his fellowservants, which owed him an hundred pence: and he laid hands on him, and took him by the throat, saying, Pay me that thou owest. And his fellowservant fell down at his feet, and besought him, saying, Have patience with me, and I will pay thee all. And he would not: but went and cast him into prison, till he should pay the debt. So when his fellowservants saw what was done, they were very sorry, and came

and told unto their lord all that was done. Then his lord, after that he had called him, said unto him, O thou wicked servant, I forgave thee all that debt, because thou desiredst me: Shouldest not thou also have had compassion on thy fellowservant, even as I had pity on thee? And his lord was wroth, and delivered him to the tormentors, till he should pay all that was due unto him. So likewise shall my heavenly Father do also unto you, if ye from your hearts forgive not every one his brother their trespasses." (Matthew 18:21-35)

In this scripture, we see Jesus make it an important priority to forgive and continue to forgive. Essentially, seventy times seven is too much to keep count. As such, we are always to forgive from the heart. Then He went on to tell about forgiveness and the kingdom of heaven. The one who did not forgive was delivered to tormentors. Does your life often seem like "hell" on earth? Maybe you go from one issue or problem to another. Many times you may bring these on to yourself, but maybe not. Hell on earth is not the kingdom of God. You have been "delivered to tormentors". There is most likely unforgiveness in your life.

2nd Samuel 13 gives us an example where ultimately unforgiveness can lead. I highly recommend you read chapters 13 through 18 of 2nd Samuel specifically in reference to this. However, I will summarize them here. The story starts in 2nd Samuel verses 1-21. Amnon, son of David, deceives and rapes his sister Tamar. Tamar's brother Absalom takes on Tamar's offense. Verse 22 shows us that this develops to the point of hate *"And Absalom spake unto his*

89

brother Amnon neither good nor bad: for Absalom hated Amnon, because he had forced his sister Tamar" (2 Samuel 13:22). We see the first step in unforgiveness is that it turns to hatred. Verses 23-33 give us the next step. Here Absalom hurts his brother Anmon. In this specific case, he actually kills him. In verses 38 and 39 we see Absalom separates himself from his father. *"So Absalom fled, and went to Geshur, and was there three years. And the soul of king David longed to go forth unto Absalom: for he was comforted concerning Amnon, seeing he was dead."* The third step in the progression of unforgiveness is that we separate ourselves, often from those who love us, and even from God our father.

In chapter 14, we see Absalom returned, but never reconciled with his father David. We also see him being destructive. In verse 30 of 2nd Samuel 14 it states *"Therefore he said unto his servants, See, Joab's field is near mine, and he hath barley there; go and set it on fire. And Absalom's servants set the field on fire."* He did this to get attention and be reconciled with his father King David. However, we never see King David, nor Absalom, ever deal with the offenses.

Chapter 15 shows the progression of pride, mixed with unforgiveness in Absalom.

> *"And it came to pass after this, that Absalom prepared him chariots and horses, and fifty men to run before him. And Absalom rose up early, and stood beside the way of the gate: and it was so, that when any man that had a controversy came to the king for judgment, then Absalom called unto him, and said, Of what city art thou? And he said, Thy servant is of one of the tribes of Israel. And Absalom said unto him, See, thy matters are good and*

right; but there is no man deputed of the king to hear thee. Absalom said moreover, Oh that I were made judge in the land, that every man which hath any suit or cause might come unto me, and I would do him justice! And it was so, that when any man came nigh to him to do him obeisance, he put forth his hand, and took him, and kissed him. And on this manner did Absalom to all Israel that came to the king for judgment: so Absalom stole the hearts of the men of Israel" (2 Samuel 15:1-6).

The following verses in chapter 15 document how Absalom stole the kingship from David. He even pulled other well meaning men into his actions.

In chapter 17, after Absalom has mostly secured power as the new king, we see the next step in the pattern of unforgiveness. We see Absalom deceived.

"Moreover Ahithophel said unto Absalom, Let me now choose out twelve thousand men, and I will arise and pursue after David this night: And I will come upon him while he is weary and weak handed, and will make him afraid: and all the people that are with him shall flee; and I will smite the king only: And I will bring back all the people unto thee: the man whom thou seekest is as if all returned: so all the people shall be in peace. And the saying pleased Absalom well, and all the elders of Israel. Then said Absalom, Call now Hushai the Archite also, and let us hear likewise what he saith. And when Hushai was come to Absalom, Absalom

spake unto him, saying, Ahithophel hath spoken after this manner: shall we do after his saying? if not; speak thou. And Hushai said unto Absalom, The counsel that Ahithophel hath given is not good at this time. For, said Hushai, thou knowest thy father and his men, that they be mighty men, and they be chafed in their minds, as a bear robbed of her whelps in the field: and thy father is a man of war, and will not lodge with the people. Behold, he is hid now in some pit, or in some other place: and it will come to pass, when some of them be overthrown at the first, that whosoever heareth it will say, There is a slaughter among the people that follow Absalom. And he also that is valiant, whose heart is as the heart of a lion, shall utterly melt: for all Israel knoweth that thy father is a mighty man, and they which be with him are valiant men. Therefore I counsel that all Israel be generally gathered unto thee, from Dan even to Beersheba, as the sand that is by the sea for multitude; and that thou go to battle in thine own person. So shall we come upon him in some place where he shall be found, and we will light upon him as the dew falleth on the ground: and of him and of all the men that are with him there shall not be left so much as one. Moreover, if he be gotten into a city, then shall all Israel bring ropes to that city, and we will draw it into the river, until there be not one small stone found there. And Absalom and all the men of

Israel said, The counsel of Hushai the Archite is better than the counsel of Ahithophel. For the LORD had appointed to defeat the good counsel of Ahithophel, to the intent that the LORD might bring evil upon Absalom" (2 Samuel 17:1-14).

The final step in unforgiveness is destruction. *"Then said Joab, I may not tarry thus with thee. And he took three darts in his hand, and thrust them through the heart of Absalom, while he was yet alive in the midst of the oak. And ten young men that bare Joab's armour compassed about and smote Absalom, and slew him"* (2nd Samuel 18:14-15) This caused further grief, and pain to those who loved him.

Unforgiveness leads to hatred. This hatred drives us to hurt others, and not necessarily the one that hurt us originally. It leads us to separation and pride. We then become open to deception. Ultimately, unforgiveness will end in destruction.

So what do you do to stop this pattern in your life? The Lord's prayer gives us the answer. Matthew 6:12 states *"And forgive us our debts, as we forgive our debtors"*. If you will do this daily, you will break the pattern of unforgiveness in your life. It is important to learn to be quick to forgive. Secondly, ask the Lord to show you your deep hurts. You will probably not get an immediate answer, but you will eventually get it answered. You may not like the way this is answered. You may have to "go through the fire" to bring many of the issues you've buried to the surface. *"Behold, I have refined thee, but not with silver; I have chosen thee in the furnace of affliction."* (Isaiah 48:10) It may be embarrassing. People might not understand. However, if you hold fast to the goal of dealing with them, it will result in a freedom you've never known. This process may take three years for the major stuff to get out as it did for me, or it may take longer. I know one person for whom this process has continued for over twelve years. Is it done? Well, until we see Jesus, we will continue to be refined. Just as we need God's righteousness everyday, we need God's healing everyday. However, there is a point where the past has been dealt with, and you can deal with the present issues of life only.

When God does show you these deep things in your life, be sure to forgive specifically. Give the hurts, wrongs and your own failures to the Lord and trust that God will work them out for good. Be sure to forgive yourself. Forgive out loud. Speak your forgiveness. When you see faults in your life, character traits and similar issues that do not reflect Jesus, realize that many, if not all of these, are a result of hurts and unforgiveness. Seek God for His answers. Determine what God's word for your situation is. Replace the lie with the truth so you can be set free.

Finally, James 5:16 states *"Confess your faults one to another, and pray one for another, that ye may be healed."* Find someone you trust that will pray with you about these things. This may be your spouse or someone else close. This is important. The rest of that same verse continues *"The effectual fervent prayer of a righteous man availeth much."* Jesus said that the devil had nothing in him. *"The prince of this world cometh, and hath nothing in me."* (John 14:30) God's desire for us is that we too are free from the devil and that he have nothing in us. We must be willing to expose the darkness within to the light of God. *"If therefore the light that is in thee be darkness, how great is that darkness!"* (Matthew 6:23). We do this by confessing our faults.

The Bible also gives us an admonition to stand fast in this freedom. Galatians 5:1 states *"Stand fast therefore in the liberty wherewith Christ hath made us free, and be not entangled again with the yoke of bondage."* This shows us that we can be bound again. Therefore, to stand, we need to understand how we got free in the first place, so that we can stay free. It is impossible to go into your promised land if you are still in bondage to Egypt.

I've spent a lot of time discussing healing of the inner man. This is where every one of us needs healing. However, God does not stop there. God wants us healed in spirit, soul, and body. Healing for our bodies is just as much a promise today as it was in Bible times. This is an area that many Christians also find hard to receive. Many people refuse to believe. Some churches have gone so far as to teach that healing is not for today. However, the word says *"For I am the LORD, I change not"* (Malachi 3:6). When Jesus was asked if He was willing to heal, He replied that He was willing. *"And, behold, there came a leper and worshipped him, saying, Lord, if thou wilt, thou canst make me clean. And Jesus put forth his hand, and touched him, saying, I will; be thou clean. And immediately his leprosy was cleansed"* (Matthew 8:2-3). Once again we see *"Jesus Christ the same yesterday, and today, and forever"* (Hebrews 13:8).

Remember, that you were not saved until *after* you believed. Your unbelief prevented your salvation. So is it with healing. Your unbelief may prevent your healing. *"And he did not many mighty works there because of their unbelief"* (Matthew 13:58). It is time to change your thinking and your belief. *"Put on the new man, which is renewed in knowledge after the image of him that created him"* (Collosians 3:10)

In 1986, I was on a trip to Maryland to visit my sister and attend my High School reunion. The flights I took included a connecting flight through Charlotte, North Carolina. As the plane left Charlotte, I noticed a pain developing in my teeth. I recognized what it was.

I had been warned of this by a dentist. My wisdom tooth was infected. This was not something good. I was on a vacation trip and sure didn't need to deal with this now, of all times. I leaned toward and looked out the window, reached my hand to my face and prayed "Oh God, please heal this infection. I'm on vacation and I don't need to deal with this now." Instantly, I felt the pain leave. God miraculously healed my wisdom tooth infection. I was so relieved. This could have really ruined my trip.

After returning home, a few weeks, or maybe even months later, I had failed to deal with this issue. Once again, I felt the same pain in my mouth building up. It was Friday night and I was visiting at Harriet's with some others. This time I prayed for it, but nothing happened. I mentioned it to Harriet and the others. Someone said I needed to see a dentist. My answer was, "Yes, but seeing a dentist is something you do on Monday morning, not Friday night." Well, by Saturday morning, the side of my face was swelled the size of a baseball. Fortunately, I was able to link up with a dentist early in the morning to deal with the infection. This eventually led to the removal of my wisdom teeth. So, for the complete healing of the cause of the problem, God used a dentist. I'm sure He could have supernaturally healed me, but He chose to have a dentist do the work. Ultimately, God was still the healer.

A number of years ago, I injured my foot playing volleyball. Then, less than a year afterwards, I reinjured it even worse while playing racquetball. Prayer didn't result in any immediate miracle. The day after the second injury I could hardly walk. I went to my doctor, who found a hairline fracture and a pretty banged up joint. Overall, however, it was not serious. He treated it with anti-inflammatory drugs and it improved rapidly. Over six months passed. The foot got better but the joint always hurt. Something was still wrong. I went back to the doctor. He sent me to a specialist.

After examination, the specialist gave me the news that I had injury induced arthritis in the joint. There was nothing he could do for me. He prescribed some anti-inflammatories and told me I would have to live with it the rest of my life. I didn't like that. I was determined to not be on drugs all the time. After the first prescription expired, I refused to renew it. God was my healer. He would heal me. My foot still hurt. I answered a prayer call for healing at my church with a visiting evangelist that said God had anointed him to heal the sick. He prayed for my foot. My foot still hurt. I claimed my healing *"With his stripes we are healed"* (Isaiah 53:5).

Every morning as I put on my shoes, I laid hands on my joint and said "Be healed in Jesus Name". I commanded the arthritis to go in Jesus name. This went on for probably 2 years. One morning, I realized my foot did not hurt anymore. I realized that it had not hurt for quite a while. I couldn't really remember the last time it hurt. The joint was normal. It has been many years since. I have not had arthritis in my foot. It does not hurt. God is my healer. My incurable disease has been cured.

By the blessing of the Lord, I have not had major challenges requiring physical miracles. I personally stand on the scripture *"The Lord will keep you free from every disease"* (Dueteronomy 7:15 NIV). Does this mean I never get sick? Apparently, I still need to learn all the conditions of this word completely (see the previous verses), because I do not walk entirely in health. I can say that God has kept me amazingly well. This week, as I began to write this chapter, I missed a day of work due to sickness for the first time in over 10 years. I expect God to keep me healthy.

I do know a number of people who have had great challenges in their physical health. My pastor testifies of being healed of cancer. I also knew a lady at a church I used to attend, that died from cancer while believing for healing. Why do some get healed and others do not? I'm not God. I can't answer that. I do not know. However, I will continue to believe God heals, whether or not it manifests. It is in the word of God, whether or not I believe it. So I choose to believe.

In Acts chapter 3 we find documented the story of a great healing at the temple in Jerusalem. It gives us something to consider relative to this question.

> *"Now Peter and John went up together into the temple at the hour of prayer, being the ninth hour. And a certain man lame from his mother's womb was carried, whom they laid daily at the gate of the temple which is called Beautiful, to ask alms of them that entered into the temple; Who seeing Peter and John about to go into the temple asked an alms. And Peter, fastening his eyes upon him with John, said, Look on us. And he gave heed unto them, expecting to receive something of them. Then Peter said, Silver and gold have I none; but such as I have give I thee: In the name of Jesus Christ of Nazareth rise up and walk. And he took him by the right hand, and lifted him up: and immediately his feet and ankle bones received strength. And he leaping up stood, and walked, and entered with them into the temple, walking, and leaping, and praising God. And all the*

*people saw him walking and praising
God: And they knew that it was he
which sat for alms at the Beautiful gate
of the temple: and they were filled with
wonder and amazement at that which
had happened unto him"* (Acts 3:1-10).

Here, Peter and John had a great miracle of healing by
faith in the name of Jesus. This miracle occurred at the
Beautiful gate of the temple. We know that Jesus
frequently visited the temple in Jerusalem. This man
was "laid daily" at this gate and was "lame from his
mother's womb". Yet, in all of Jesus' visits, this man
was never healed by Jesus. Why? Jesus said *"For I
came down from heaven, not to do mine own will, but
the will of him that sent me"* (John 6:38). This too
must be our goal, to do the will of him that sends us. If
we are truly walking in His will, we too will see His
miracles of healing

Healing the sick is something that is the will of
God for us to do. Jesus gave a command to his
disciples to heal the sick. *"Heal the sick, cleanse the
lepers, raise the dead, cast out devils: freely ye have
received, freely give"* (Matthew 10:8). If we are to be
disciples of Christ, we need to follow His command.

I have had the privilege of being personally
involved in some of God's miracles. The Bible says
*"And these signs shall follow them that believe; In my
name shall they cast out devils; they shall speak with
new tongues; They shall take up serpents; and if they
drink any deadly thing, it shall not hurt them; they
shall lay hands on the sick, and they shall recover"*
(Mark 16:17-18). I'd like to share a few of them here.

It was probably 1987 or so. I was working at
Texas Instruments. I had the privilege of leading a
coworker named Michelle to salvation through sharing
with her the message of the Lord's Prayer. One day as
we went to lunch, she said to me something to the

effect of "You seem to have most of the same kinds of issues that I do, but you seem to deal with them so much better. How do you do it?"

"I pray" was my answer.

"Does it work?" she replied.

"Absolutely, you should try it."

"But how?"

I shared with her the Lord's Prayer as an outline, and promised to bring her a set of tapes to listen to on the subject. I brought them the next day. Four days later she came to me excited. She said she felt so much better. She was off her tranquilizers and no longer had to see her psychiatrist. Prayer was really working. I also can testify that I saw her life change thereafter. She also got saved through this.

Some months later, Michelle and I went to lunch again. She was rather distressed. Something was really bothering her. She told me that the doctor said she had some disease of the eyes and was going blind. The doctor said that they could not cure it. I don't remember the name of the disease. She told me to look at her eyes. There were strange yellow growths in them. They did not look healthy. When we returned from lunch and pulled into the parking space, I reached over, laid my hand across her eyes and said something like "Eyes be healed in Jesus name." It was just a short prayer. I then told her to read her Bible about the fig tree that Jesus cursed, that was found the next day dried from the roots.

That evening driving home from work, as I was praying, the Lord spoke to me and told me that He had healed Michelle's eyes. I was excited. I knew that I had heard from God. I got home and called Michelle and told her what God said. She was not enthusiastic. She did not hear God say this. Things looked the same to her. However, over the next few days her eyes cleared up. She went back to the doctor. She was healed!

One of the best things about this testimony is what happened next as relayed to me by Michelle. Michelle was big into working out. She and her fiancé were running at some track with someone else they knew. This man hurt his ankle, apparently rather badly. Michelle went over and put her hand on his ankle and said "In Jesus name be healed". The pain left. The ankle was healed! The man looked at her in amazement. After being healed, he did not know what to think. His next words were "You're weird". Just the same, he was healed! I assure you that a seed for the Gospel was planted in that man. Michelle had become a believer in healing, and these signs were following her. They can follow you too.

Another amazing thing happened with my friend Rose Marie. I met Rose Marie at a home care group for singles. She was an older lady, probably at least 15 years, if not more, older than I. She visited our home care group that night, for the first, and possibly the last time. I don't remember for sure. During the prayer time that night, when people asked for prayer, she came forward and said that she was visiting her son and daughter-in-law. She said she was a manic depressive and that her prescription had run out. She could not refill it without going back to Louisiana. She was scared.

As most of the people in the care group went forward to pray for her, I held back. As they were nearing completion I felt led of the Spirit to pray for her. I went forward, took her by the hands, and said commandingly "In the name of Jesus, you spirit of depression go." Something that felt like electricity went through me, through my arms and hands to Rose Marie. She collapsed under the power of the Spirit into the chair behind her. As she got up a number of minutes later, she was free and she knew it. I knew it too. I had felt God's power go through me. I can't say that this usually happens when I pray for people. Usually it does not. This time it did.

After that, Rose Marie and I became closer friends. I linked her up with another of my friends to pick her up and get her to the rather powerful Friday morning prayer meetings that were going on at my church during that time. I also attended, but it was much out of my way to pick her up. She also attended a couple of the Saturday morning praise and worship sessions. Soon, the time came that she had to go back to her home in Louisiana. We kept in touch by phone occasionally.

Some time later, I received a call from Rose Marie. She was in the hospital somewhere in Louisiana. Something had happened and she was paralyzed from the waist down. She asked for prayer. The doctors did not think she would ever walk again. We talked for a while. I promised to pray for her and hung up.

The following Saturday morning after my morning praise and worship time, I felt led of the Spirit to call Rose Marie at the hospital. She answered the phone and the conversation went something like this (these are not exact quotes - but very similar):

"Oh brother, it's so good to hear from you. I was hoping that you would call."

"Well, I knew it was time to call you," I replied, "How are you doing?"

"Considering the circumstances, I'm okay I guess. But, oh darn, I have something I wanted to share with you," Rose Marie said.

"What's the matter? Why can't you share it?" I answered.

"It's in my Bible, which is on the other side of the room, and the nurse is not here. I can't get it." She continued.

"Well you'll just have to go get it yourself," I said, matter of factly, paused for a moment, then continued, "In Jesus name, stand up."

Noise on the other end of the phone. "I'm still standin' brother," she said.

"In Jesus name, walk" I told her.

I hear the phone get put down. I hear movement across the floor. A voice calls out to me from the other side of the room, rather excitedly, "I'm at the other side of the room, and I'm still standing up!"

Back in my apartment, I was practically bouncing off the ceiling. God had just healed a paralyzed woman a few hundred miles away as I talked to her on the phone! It was exciting! I had never been this close to a physical miracle of this magnitude. She returned to the phone, and our conversation continued for a while before it was time to go. I don't remember any of the details, but I was excited!

A few days later she shared with me what happened next. After she hung up the phone, she walked down the hall to the nurse's station. The nurse that saw her was so startled she said to her "You can't do that!" Obviously, she could, and already had! The hospital had a doctor in to examine her, ran some tests, and let her go home within a day or so. It was a true miracle they could not explain.

Rose Marie has since gone on to be with the Lord, but I will never forget her. This experience confirmed in me that there is nothing that the Lord can't heal. Sometimes, He does it in awesome miracles that stun and amaze us. Other times, the healing takes place over time, with no fanfare at all. Our part is to believe the word of God, stand on it, and act on it. God is the healer. Sickness, disease, hurts and offenses are not part of the Kingdom of God.

Healing goes beyond just ourselves. As I have testified to some of the miracles I've seen God do, these did not all affect me only. As we take our promised land, we will take others with us. God will heal our families, our friends, and our land.

"Beloved, I wish above all things that thou mayest prosper and be in health, even as thy soul prospereth."
(3 John 1:2)

Questions for consideration or discussion

1. Have you experienced God as your healer in your own life? Give examples.

2. Do you find that there are situations that you react rather than respond to? Give examples.

3. Do you ever feel that you don't measure up or are not "good enough"? When and how?

4. Are there issues from your past that seem insurmountable to you? Explain.

5. Can you say in all honesty that you really like who you are? Why or why not?

6. Do you seem at times to be in torment from people, situations, or emotionally? Does life sometimes seem like hell on earth? Explain.

7. Have you ever asked God to show you your deep hurts, with the intent of trusting God to heal you of them and set you free? If not, are you ready to ask Him now?

8. Are there people that you need to forgive? Who?

9. Who is in your life that you can be honest and open with and "pray that you may be healed"?

10. Have you ever seen or personally experienced physical miracles? Give examples.

11. Are you ready to receive Jesus as the healer of your physical body?

12. Are you willing to step out and boldly pray for the sick to be healed? And expect God to actually heal them?

Chapter 9
It's Not About Money
The Lord Our Provider

"For the love of money is the root of all evil: which while some coveted after, they have erred from the faith, and pierced themselves through with many sorrows." (1 Timothy 6:10)

The biggest stumbling block for most believers preventing them from entering the kingdom of God is money. Wouldn't you like to be able to never worry about money again? Sure you say, just give me a few million dollars and I'm there. I can assure you that would not do it. You'd probably spend your time worrying about not losing those millions or worrying if it was enough. The kingdom of God is a *better* deal. Jesus said *"Take no thought, saying, What shall we eat? or, What shall we drink? or, Wherewithal shall we be clothed? (For after all these things do the Gentiles seek:) for your heavenly Father knoweth that ye have need of all these things. But seek ye first the kingdom of God, and his righteousness; and all these things shall be added unto you."* (Matthew 6:31-33) For those that seek Him, He will freely give all things. Romans 8:32 says *"He that spared not his own Son, but delivered him up for us all, how shall he not with him also freely give us all things?"*

Does this sound like a good deal? It should, because it is. However, it is often hard to receive this. First, we don't receive it because we don't really know the giver. Second, we don't know His ways when it comes to money. I remember speaking to someone about ten years ago about God as provider. This person seemed to be a pretty solid Christian. However, when I started talking about the tithe and God providing, he stated rather factually "I don't believe that way." My

106

attempts to discuss this further went nowhere. He had already been preconditioned to not believe.

To be honest, I can understand why, at least to a point. This has been an area where I have heard much unbalanced teaching in the church, generally from some very well meaning preachers (although as Christians we really should study God's word on this for ourselves). There are basically two teachings that drive Christians away from God's truth about money. The first of these is usually cloaked in "religion". It teaches the church a poverty mentality. This is the mentality that it is somehow spiritual to be poor, or do without. For those who are poor and do without, this becomes a badge that is also a trap that can prevent them from getting free from poverty.

One scripture seems to be used more than any other to justify this position. This is the scripture in Matthew 8:20 and repeated in Luke 9:58 that says *"And Jesus said unto him, Foxes have holes, and birds of the air have nests; but the Son of man hath not where to lay his head."* (Luke 9:58). I have heard this scripture used many times to justify that Jesus did not have a home. It makes Him sound homeless. Aside from the fact that I've never met anyone who would follow a homeless man, and multitudes followed Jesus, this is just not supported by scripture.

First, we need to understand the context of statement. Luke 9:51-53 gives us this context *"And it came to pass, when the time was come that he should be received up, he stedfastly set his face to go to Jerusalem, And sent messengers before his face: and they went, and entered into a village of the Samaritans, to make ready for him. And they did not receive him, because his face was as though he would go to Jerusalem."* This shows us that He was rejected by the Samaritans. This is a long way from Capernaum in Galilee, where the Bible says Jesus lived. *"And*

107

leaving Nazareth, he came and dwelt in Capernaum" (Matthew 4:13). So no place to lay his head was because He was away from his home, not because He was homeless. This is further confirmed in John 1:38-39 *"Then Jesus turned, and saw them following, and saith unto them, What seek ye? They said unto him, Rabbi, (which is to say, being interpreted, Master,) where dwellest thou? He saith unto them, Come and see. They came and saw where he dwelt, and abode with him that day: for it was about the tenth hour."* This clearly shows that Jesus had a place that he lived. Mark 2:1-4 further confirms and clarifies that this place was a house *"And again he entered into Capernaum after some days; and it was noised that he was **in the house**. And straightway many were gathered together, insomuch that there was no room to receive them, no, not so much as about the door: and he preached the word unto them. And they come unto him, bringing one sick of the palsy, which was borne of four. And when they could not come nigh unto him for the press, they uncovered the roof where he was: and when they had broken it up, they let down the bed wherein the sick of the palsy lay"* (emphasis added).

Obviously, nothing in these scriptures tells us that He owned the house, nor do they say that He did not. Although I could make an unprovable argument that He probably owned the house, whether He did or not is not really important to this discussion. Jesus had that which He needed, a place to live. This is a key point that God took care of him, just as He will take care of you. You do not have to worry.

Along these same lines recently I heard what I consider to be one of the ultimate dumb questions. "What would Jesus drive?" This was a ploy by a certain group to push their agenda for more environmentally conscious automobiles. However, it got a lot of publicity and was a subject for discussion on Christian talk radio. What amazed me, listening to this on Christian talk radio, were the answers I heard. First of all the question in itself is ludicrous, because Jesus walked this earth during an age where there were no automobiles at all. So the real answer was that He wouldn't drive anything, because there was nothing for Him to drive. Interestingly enough, I never even heard this answer given by any of the callers on the radio! I heard quite a few answers that said He would walk, take the bus, and similar. Not one caller realized that if Jesus were walking this earth as a man today, God would have provided whatever Jesus needed. If Jesus needed a bus, He would have had a bus. If He needed an airplane, He would have had an airplane. God would see that He would have whatever He needed. That's the point. God provides our needs if we trust Him and let Him.

Interestingly enough, even though many Christians have at least partially "bought into" this poverty mentality, I don't really see anyone live it. People who defend this are not rushing out to give away their entire earthly possessions (house, car, clothes, etc.) so they can live in the poverty that they claim is spiritual and be "like Jesus". What I do see is many Christians who have been fed this poverty mentality, make a decision that they are not going to live like that (in poverty). So when the church leadership talks to them about tithes and offerings, they subconsciously equate giving to "losing" and lack, rather than blessing and reject it. Remember *"It is more blessed to give than to receive"* (Acts 20:35).

Another scripture that is often used to substantiate the poverty mentality claim is Mark 10:17-23.

> *"And when he was gone forth into the way, there came one running, and kneeled to him, and asked him, Good*

Master, what shall I do that I may inherit eternal life? And Jesus said unto him, Why callest thou me good? there is none good but one, that is, God. Thou knowest the commandments, Do not commit adultery, Do not kill, Do not steal, Do not bear false witness, Defraud not, Honour thy father and mother. And he answered and said unto him, Master, all these have I observed from my youth. Then Jesus beholding him loved him, and said unto him, One thing thou lackest: go thy way, sell whatsoever thou hast, and give to the poor, and thou shalt have treasure in heaven: and come, take up the cross, and follow me. And he was sad at that saying, and went away grieved: for he had great possessions. And Jesus looked round about, and saith unto his disciples, How hardly shall they that have riches enter into the kingdom of God!"

The problem here is that to get the full picture you need to include verses 24 through 30 which state:

*"And the disciples were astonished at his words. But Jesus answereth again, and saith unto them, Children, how hard is it for them that **trust in riches** to enter into the kingdom of God! It is easier for a camel to go through the eye of a needle, than for a rich man to enter into the kingdom of God. And they were astonished out of measure, saying among themselves, Who then can be saved? And Jesus looking upon them saith, With men it is impossible, but not*

110

with God: for with God all things are possible. Then Peter began to say unto him, Lo, we have left all, and have followed thee. And Jesus answered and said, Verily I say unto you, There is no man that hath left house, or brethren, or sisters, or father, or mother, or wife, or children, or lands, for my sake, and the gospel's, But he shall receive an hundredfold now in this time, houses, and brethren, and sisters, and mothers, and children, and lands, with persecutions; and in the world to come eternal life" (emphasis added).

Here we see a few things that clarify this. First, Jesus specifically clarifies that it is those who "trust in riches", not just have them, that have a problem entering the kingdom of God. (Remember, we have shown that the kingdom of God is not just for heaven, but also for here on earth. This is not talking only about salvation.) Jesus also stated that for those who had "left all" to follow him, they would receive *"an hundredfold now in this time"*.

This is where we get into the other teaching that gets Christians off track. This is what I call the "prosperity Gospel". Although I believe that God desires to prosper his people, and I can back it up with many scriptures, there is often a missing balance in this teaching. The problem is a focus on "getting" (the hundred fold), rather than on the kingdom of God. The kingdom of God is not about money! This is something else that keeps Christians away from God's truth about money and provision. It also drives away nonbelievers since those who preach this "prosperity Gospel" appear to the lost, and to many in the church, as "out for money" or "always asking for money". As I share my testimony following, I hope to bring you to a place where you can best understand this balance.

One day, over 14 years ago now, I prayed the Lord's Prayer as an outline, the same as I have been sharing through this book. As I prayed "Hallowed be thy name" and hallowed the covenant names of God, this is what I prayed (very close to word for word). "Father in heaven, I really know you as Jehovah-tsidkenu, the Lord my Righteousness. And I really know you as Jehovah-m'kaddesh, the Lord who sanctifies me. And I thank you Lord, that I really know you as Jehovah-shalom, my peace. And Lord you really are Jehovah-shammah, the Lord who is present with me. Lord, I also know you really are my healer, Jehovah-rophe. And Lord, I know that you are my banner, Jehovah-nissi, who fights for me. And I know you as Jehovah-rohi, my shepherd, who really does lead me and guide me in paths of righteousness. But Lord, I don't really know you as my provider. I trust you as my provider, but I really don't know you as my provider. Lord, I want to know you as my provider." I believe this prayer started a chain of events in my life that took me to the place that I can really say I *know* the Lord is my provider.

For quite some time before this, I had been praying for and asking the Lord for a specific new keyboard for my music. I wanted a Roland RD-300 Digital Electric Piano. It was about the best electronic piano you could buy at the time, at least in my opinion. A few weeks after I had prayed the prayer above, I got the release in my spirit to actually buy the keyboard. It was not cheap. Between the keyboard, a new stand, and a quality road case, the total was somewhere above $3,000.00. It pretty much wiped out my savings.

No more than a few weeks after I had done this, the Lord told me to marry Angel. (I shared this story in chapter 5.) However, now I really didn't have any money saved up, since I had just spent my savings on a keyboard. Getting married was not in my plans at the time. I did what I felt I had to do, and purchased her engagement and wedding ring on a credit card. This was as far in the hole as I could comfortably go. I did not have any money for a honeymoon. I shared this with Angel. We sat on the floor in the living room of my apartment and agreed in prayer. We told the Lord that we would like to have a honeymoon, but didn't have any money for it.

During our prayer time, the Lord spoke to me and told me we would have a honeymoon. I shared this with Angel and we started planning for it, even though we had no idea how we would pay for it. In the week before our wedding, Angel's grandmother came to visit and spend the week with Angel. On Thursday night, the three of us were in my apartment, sitting at the dining room table. I was at the head of the table, Angel's grandmother was on my right, and Angel was on my left. Angel's grandmother said to us "I want to give you your wedding present tonight."

She pulled out her checkbook and began to write a check. We weren't expecting much. Grandma lived on social security and was not in any way a woman of "means". She finished writing the check and put it on the place mat in front of me. I briefly glanced at it, and put it on Angel's place mat.

Angel glanced at the check and continued to talk, with a brief "thank you" to her Grandmother. I touched Angel on the arm and said, "Angel, you need to look at that check again." She looked at it, realized the amount, and then I heard a more appropriate response. Originally, Angel had thought the check was for $100.00. It was actually for $1,000.00, which was a very big gift from Grandma! I said to Angel, "We'll have that honeymoon we planned!"

For our wedding that following Saturday, we received an additional couple of hundred dollars in wedding gifts. These enabled us to pay for all the costs of the wedding almost to the penny. The thousand dollar gift covered our honeymoon. God had provided.

We had only been married three weeks when Angel got pregnant! We had discussed wanting to have children and were not going to do anything to prevent it, but three weeks was mighty fast. We had expected to have to try for a couple of months. Now, we already had a baby on the way.

I didn't like the idea of raising children in an apartment. In my mind, a house was a much better environment. I reviewed my financial situation in detail. I went over it with Angel one Tuesday night. I showed her the situation we were in. By my best estimate, the soonest we could consider buying a house was at least one year away. This bugged me. I really didn't like this. I wanted to have a house to raise my children in.

During that time, I worked for Texas Instruments. I had two offices, one at the Dallas Expressway site, and one in Lewisville, Texas. I would often stop at a park in Carrollton, Texas, approximately midway between these two offices to eat my lunch. Thursday of that same week, I stopped there. I was thinking about my situation with the baby coming and being stuck in an apartment. I was as much talking to myself about it as I was to God. However, the Lord spoke to me and said "Buy a house." I had no doubt that He had spoken to me, and no doubt what He had said. However, I sure could not see how I could possibly do this.

For the next four or five hours of the day, while at work and driving home, I continued to tell God why I couldn't do what He said. I told Him all the reasons I could not afford it. I told Him that I had just evaluated our finances and there was no way. However, I really knew God had spoken to me to do this.

When I got home, I told Angel God had told me to buy a house. She looked at me rather incredulously and said, "You just showed me how impossible that is."

"I know, but God told me to buy a house. Let's pray", I replied.

Once more, we sat in the middle of the living room and agreed in prayer about this word from God. When we got up from prayer, Angel agreed, "I think we really *are* supposed to buy a house."

We proceeded to make a list of things we wanted in a house. We divided a piece of paper in half. On the left side of the paper we listed the things we absolutely needed to have in a house. On the right hand side of the paper, we listed the things we wanted to have in a house, beyond the needs. After we made the list, we decided to pray in agreement over it. Once again, we sat in the middle of the living room floor and prayed. We submitted our list to God.

One thing I had known for some time was that when I actually did move, I felt the Lord had told me I would move to Rockwall, about 10 miles east of where my apartment was, and the same town where my church was located. I shared this with Angel and told her that I knew of a place in Rockwall where they were building new homes. They were little dinky homes, that really wouldn't meet our needs, but I figured we could go there on Saturday and check them out. This way we could get some idea of what houses cost in Rockwall and see what we were up against.

On Saturday, we checked out these new homes. It turned out that they were no longer building little dinky homes like I had visited in the past, but rather some reasonable sized decent homes. We looked at models, plans and houses under construction. We found one plan that really worked well for us. It was everything we needed and virtually everything we had on our wish list of wants also. However, it was almost $30,000 more than what I could even stretch my imagination to be able to afford.

On Sunday, after church, we hooked up with a real estate agent and looked at previously owned homes in Rockwall. People were proud of their houses. These houses cost even more than the new construction. There were not many available, and not one that we looked at would even come close to what we really wanted. It seemed that the new construction was the way to go, but how would we afford it?

Once again, we agreed in prayer. I had a VA loan available, so a down payment wasn't a problem. However, everything else was, including the monthly mortgage payment. Additionally, we would need all those things that are needed for a home, that are not needed in an apartment. Some of these are expensive, such as a refrigerator and lawn mower. Other similar things like window blinds and curtains, and lawn tools, also add up.

We also had other concerns. We had a baby coming. I had insurance from my job, but it did not cover everything. I was going to end up needing to pay the hospital close to $1000.00 above the insurance payments when the baby was born. We picked the house plan that met all of our needs, and the vast majority of the things we wanted above our minimum needs. It was way more than I thought I could afford. No matter how I calculated it, I did not see how we could afford to buy this house. However, I had peace and we both felt it was God leading us to do this. One week from the day that God spoke to me to buy a house, we signed a contract to have one built. I put down $500.00 in earnest money. We had approximately six months for the house to be built.

116

We decided to agree in prayer about all these things. We asked God to provide for the closing costs, moving expenses, hospital expenses and all the things we would need for a house. We had some specific requests. We asked the Lord that by the time the baby was born, that we would not only be moved in to our new house, and have the things we needed to do that, but that we would have cash to pay off the hospital bill and be able to pay off my car, which would have had another six months or so of additional payments remaining. We also prayed and asked God that when the baby was born, that Angel would not have to work, that we could live off of my salary alone.

During this time, I was determined to trust God for provision. I had been tithing consistently for a couple of years by this time and I was also giving a significant offering above and beyond the tithe. I had committed $20.00 per week to a building fund program and was actually doubling that pledge. It was a significant amount of money to us, but it was what we believed God had told us to do.

Things went from impossible to worse. Angel, who was working as a hairstylist during this time, gets fired for her Christian witness. She really didn't do anything and what her boss did was absolutely illegal. On top of that he refused to pay her a few hundred dollars that he owed her. We could easily have taken this man to court and it would have been no contest. However, the Lord gave me a scripture, Proverbs 29:9 (NIV) *"If a wise man goes to court with a fool, the fool rages and scoffs, and there is no peace."* To me, this was a clear word from God not to take this man to court. God would take care of it.

When Angel lost her job, I struggled. I took on a burden about this house. It really bothered me and I could not let it rest. I prayed about it. I struggled about it. I acted like it was my responsibility to buy this house. It took two to three weeks before I could let go of this burden and give it to God. Finally, it didn't matter anymore. I had rest. I had given this to God.

When I finally had rest, then Angel took the burden. She could not lay it down, same as I had done. She carried this burden for another two to three weeks. Finally, she was also able to lay it down. I said to her, "It really doesn't matter. God is the one that told us to buy a house. He is the one that has to pay for it. We can't afford it whether or not you have a job."

The "naysayers" seemed to show up all over. Well-meaning Christians told me to "just quit giving in the offering." This was not something I could do in good faith. God had led me to give this amount in the offering. He had also told me to buy a house. When He told me to buy a house, He did not tell me to stop giving. I was determined to follow God. Besides this, I couldn't "make it" anyway. It was going to take God's intervention for me to be able to move into this house.

Finding a job when you are five months pregnant is particularly difficult. Even though no one can legally discriminate against you, it is pretty obvious that your priorities could easily be elsewhere. Finally, after being out of work for almost two months, Angel got a new job (after we had both laid down the burden). She got a job as a secretary for an accounting firm. The job paid about half of what she made as a hairstylist. However, everything else about the job was better. It had better and consistent daytime hours with no weekends. It did not require her to stand up all day. It did not require her to listen to awful music all day. It was a much better working environment, particularly for a pregnant woman.

On February 8, 1990, we closed on our new house in the afternoon. That very morning I got a $280.00 per month raise. "Somehow", though I never could really figure out how, we had the money for the closing costs and moving expenses. God had also given me some "tax wisdom" that saved me an additional $100.00 per month. Between the changes to my taxes and the raise, compared to the apartment costs, I was ahead on a monthly basis. God had miraculously provided!

Angel quit her job at the beginning of May. The baby was due in a week. On May 7, 1990, my daughter Stephanie was born. I paid off the hospital, writing a check for the full amount. I then went home and wrote a check for the balance owed on my car. God had answered every prayer we prayed.

Things were calm for a few months, but 1990 was a recession year. The iron curtain had come down, and defense cuts were major. In July, I was called into my boss's office. He told me that he needed to promote me. Instead, however, he told that in 60 days I would be on the surplus list. In other words, I was going to get laid off. My boss was nearly in tears. I had peace. I had joy. This was okay by me. I *knew* that God was my provider. It would work out. I didn't know how, but I had real faith in God to provide.

I had no savings to fall back on. Eight weeks severance pay was all there was. After that, I had to have a job. Jobs were not easy to find. I felt very strongly that it was not God's will for me to move. I did not even consider any interview opportunities that were out of town.

I was fortunate to land an interview very quickly with DSC Communications. I felt sure that I would get a job offer. However, weeks went by and it never came. I struggled to even get an interview. At one point, I prayed earnestly that God would give me an interview, any interview, so that I could at least have some hope. He answered that prayer with an interview at a company in Ennis, Texas, 50 miles away.

I interviewed and was offered a job. However, I just could not take it. Aside from being 50 miles away, it was just not the right job for me. I had no peace about it. I also felt that I would be very bored with the job rather quickly.

Time was running out. One Wednesday morning I spent at least an hour in prayer agonizing over this issue with God. I told God I *had* to have a job that week. There was no other option. After praying, I went out to my living room and sat down on my lawn chair to read my Bible. (I didn't have a sofa in my living room, just a lawn chair. We had been praying for a rather large and expensive sofa that we wanted but could not afford.) As I opened my Bible, God gave me scriptures out of 1 or 2 Kings that spoke to me. I don't remember the exact scriptures, but the message to me was "because you depended on me, I will deliver you". I had peace.

The following morning I had a rather unusual phone call. The personnel guy from DSC Communications that I had interviewed with weeks earlier called me and after introducing himself started the conversation like this, "You're never going to believe this."

"What am I not going to believe?" I answered.

"Well, I'm calling to offer you a job, just like you asked for, but you're never going to believe this!" He continued.

"What am I not going to believe?" I repeated.

"Well, you know corporate America, right? You know that you can't hire anyone without an approved job requisition, right? Well, I don't have one, but I'm offering you a job anyway. The CEO called me personally this morning and told me to hire you. Apparently, he and John Spencer, the guy you are going to work for, talked about you in a bar over a drink last night. He called me this morning and told me to hire you. I don't have a personnel requisition. Amazing, huh?"

"It's definitely different" I answered.

We discussed details of the job offer and he asked me when I could start, assuming I would take the job. I told him I could start Monday. He said I had to pass a drug test at a physician first. I told him I'd be glad to do that Friday. Plan for me to arrive on Monday.

As it turned out, I had one severance check left from Texas Instruments. The pay periods for DSC Communications were different. As such, I would actually get overlapping paychecks. I would essentially have an extra check. I could buy that sofa we had been praying for! We went to the local Levitz, where we had seen the sofa. This was not your average sofa. It actually was the most expensive model in the store. It was a large sectional, with a queen size sleeper section in it and recliners at both ends.

When we went to purchase it, it was on a clearance sale. However, the price was $100.00 more than the advertised sale price from about 9 months earlier when we had first seen it advertised. (We had saved the advertisement to pray over.) I told the salesman I wanted to buy that sofa, but I didn't want to pay that price. He rolled his eyes at me and said "It's on clearance." In other words, don't expect a lower price. However, I told him I would pay $100 less, since that is what it had been advertised for just a few months ago. He rather skeptically went off to discuss this with his management. About five minutes later, he returned and sold me the sofa at my price!

During all of this time, I never quit giving. I also never missed a paycheck. My drive to work was shorter with my new job. God even worked it out to answer a prayer for a new sofa that we needed. This was not an easy time. However, God showed himself to be faithful. He has proven to me that He is my provider and I can now say that I *know* him as provider. This testimony does not stop here. It could go on until this present day. God continues to provide for me time and time again.

How do you get to know God this way? First, you have to make a decision to trust Him to be who He says He is, your provider. You do this by giving and obeying God's word in giving, for *"faith without works, is dead"* (James 2:20). You trust Him by giving according to His word no matter what things look like in the natural. To do this, you have to know what God's word is in this area.

Giving according to God's work includes both tithes and offerings. Malachi 3:8-12 says *"Will a man rob God? Yet ye have robbed me. But ye say, Wherein have we robbed thee? In tithes and offerings. Ye are cursed with a curse: for ye have robbed me, even this whole nation. Bring ye all the tithes into the storehouse, that there may be meat in mine house, and prove me now herewith, saith the LORD of hosts, if I will not open you the windows of heaven, and pour you out a blessing, that there shall not be room enough to receive it. And I will rebuke the devourer for your sakes, and he shall not destroy the fruits of your ground; neither shall your vine cast her fruit before the time in the field, saith the LORD of hosts. And all nations shall call you blessed: for ye shall be a delightsome land, saith the LORD of hosts."* This is the place that we start, by trusting God in tithes and offerings.

The word tithe means tenth. The Bible makes it clear, the tithe, or tenth, is the Lord's. *"And all the tithe of the land, whether of the seed of the land, or of the fruit of the tree, is the LORD'S: it is holy unto the LORD"* (Leviticus 27:30). There are those that claim that the tithe is part of the law and no longer applies.

However, the tithe came *before* the law. Abraham gave tithes to Melchizedek king of Salem, *"And he gave him tithes of all."* (Genesis 14:20) Jesus himself confirmed the tithe when He said *"Woe unto you, scribes and Pharisees, hypocrites! for ye pay tithe of mint and anise and cummin, and have omitted the weightier matters of the law, judgment, mercy, and faith: these ought ye to have done, **and not to leave the other undone.**"* (Matthew 23:23 emphasis added).

You might say, "I can't afford to tithe." Of course you can't! If you haven't been tithing, you are under a curse. This curse is what is making it so you can't afford it. However, if you want to be free from the curse, and start receiving God's blessing, you need to tithe. If you don't tithe and give offerings and trust God to be your provider, you will never know God as your provider and you will never enter your promised land.

It is also important to understand that the tithe is *not* an offering. Malachi 3:8, stated above, distinctly separates tithes *and* offerings. The tithe provides for the church (*"meat in mine house"*), *"opens the windows of heaven"* (Malachi 3:10) and *"rebukes the devourer"* (Malachi 3:12). There are also required offerings.

What kind of offerings does God expect? There are four types of offerings in scripture that are not directly related to the tabernacle and Levitical priesthood. These offering are the freewill offering, the alms offering, the first fruits offering and what I'll call the "missions" offering. The missions offering is an offering given specifically for those that preach the gospel. (See 1 Corinthians 9:14).

The freewill offering is an offering given entirely from a willing heart *"Take ye from among you an offering unto the LORD: whosoever is of a willing heart, let him bring it, an offering of the LORD; gold, and silver, and brass"* (Exodus 35:5). You should not be coerced into giving a freewill offering.

Secondly, the freewill offering is an offering that is given in accordance with your vow or promise (if you made one), such as my building fund offering that I previously mentioned. *"That which is gone out of thy lips thou shalt keep and perform; even a freewill offering, according as thou hast vowed unto the LORD thy God, which thou hast promised with thy mouth"* (Deuteronomy 23:23) It is important to note that when you make a vow or promise, God considers it critical that we keep it, just as He keeps His promises to us. *"If a man vow a vow unto the LORD, or swear an oath to bind his soul with a bond; he shall not break his word, he shall do according to all that proceedeth out of his mouth."* (Numbers 30:2)

Finally, the freewill offering is to go to your church, the "house of God", specifically the one that you attend. *"And whosoever remaineth in any place where he sojourneth, let the men of his place help him with silver, and with gold, and with goods, and with beasts, beside the freewill offering for the house of God that is in Jerusalem."* (Ezra 1:4) *Also Ezra 7:16 states "And all the silver and gold that thou canst find in all the province of Babylon, with the freewill offering of the people, and of the priests, offering willingly for the house of their God which is in Jerusalem"*

Another offering that God expects is an alms offering, which is for the poor. Galatians 2:10 states *"Only they would that we should remember the poor; the same which I also was forward to do"*. The alms offering makes all things clean to you. *"But rather give alms of such things as ye have; and, behold, all things are clean unto you."* (Luke 11:41) When you give an alms offering, you store up for yourself treasure in the heavens. *"Sell that ye have, and give alms; provide yourselves bags which wax not old, a treasure in the heavens that faileth not, where no thief approacheth, neither moth corrupteth."* (Luke 12:33) Finally, the Lord says that when you give to the poor, He will repay you. *"He that hath pity upon the poor lendeth unto the LORD; and that which he hath given will he pay him again"* (Proverbs 19:17)

Another offering that is required is the first fruits offering. Three scriptures specifically support this. First, *"The first of the firstfruits of thy land thou shalt bring into the house of the LORD thy God"* (Exodus 23:19). Second, *"The firstfruit also of thy corn, of thy wine, and of thine oil, and the first of the fleece of thy sheep, shalt thou give him"* (Deuteronomy 18:4). Finally Nehemiah 10:35 states *"And to bring the firstfruits of our ground, and the firstfruits of all fruit of all trees, year by year, unto the house of the LORD."*

The tithe is not the first fruits offering. I have heard a number of Christians confused on this. Nehemiah 10:37 distinctly separates these two, *"And that we should bring the **firstfruits** of our dough, and our offerings, and the fruit of all manner of trees, of wine and of oil, unto the priests, to the chambers of the house of our God; **and the tithes** of our ground unto the Levites, that the same Levites might have the tithes in all the cities of our tillage"* (emphasis added). You can also see from this that the first fruits offering goes to the same place that your tithe goes, the local church.

The first fruit offering has some other benefits. First, it makes all your income holy. Romans 11:16 states *"For if the firstfruit be holy, the lump is also holy: and if the root be holy, so are the branches."* Secondly, the first fruit offering brings the increase. *"Honour the LORD with thy substance, and with the firstfruits of all thine increase: So shall thy barns be filled with plenty, and thy presses shall burst out with new wine.* " (Proverbs 3:9-10) Note also, the first fruits is given "of your increase".

For quite a number of years, when I was given a raise on my job, when I received the first paycheck with this increase, I would give the increase from the first check as an offering. Specifically, I would take the difference between my old paycheck and my new paycheck, and give that amount as an offering. This was something I felt was the right thing to do. I did not understand that what I was doing had a scriptural basis. I was giving a first fruits offering, but did not realize it.

One year, when I got a pay raise, I did not continue this practice. I was already giving offerings well above the tithe and figured I was already giving enough. About two to three months later, a visiting preacher to my church spoke on the first fruits offering. I was convicted. I realized that I had not given a first fruits offering for that pay raise. I repented and immediately gave a belated first fruits offering. I now understand the first fruits offering and will not miss it again!

The final required offering is what I have called the missions offering. This offering is specifically for those who preach the gospel. *"If we have sown unto you spiritual things, is it a great thing if we shall reap your carnal things? If others be partakers of this power over you, are not we rather? Nevertheless we have not used this power; but suffer all things, lest we should hinder the gospel of Christ. Do ye not know that they which minister about holy things live of the things of the temple? and they which wait at the altar are partakers with the altar? Even so hath the Lord ordained that they which preach the gospel should live of the gospel"* (1 Corinthians 9:11-14).

As with the other offerings, there are promises of God associated with this offering. This offering concerns both giving *and* receiving. It is well pleasing to God, and fruit will abound to your account. This is the offering, that if you give it, God promises to meet all your needs. *"Now ye Philippians know also, that in the beginning of the gospel, when I departed from Macedonia, no church communicated with me as concerning giving and receiving, but ye only. For even in Thessalonica ye sent once and again unto my necessity. Not because I desire a gift: but I desire fruit that may abound to your account. But I have all, and abound: I am full, having received of Epaphroditus the things which were sent from you, an odour of a sweet smell, a sacrifice acceptable, wellpleasing to God. But my God shall supply all your need according to his riches in glory by Christ Jesus"* (Philippians 4:15-19).

Now that we understand what the offerings are and why to give them, it's important that we understand how to give and what or how much to give. Giving should be a blessing to you. Acts 20:35 says *"I have shewed you all things, how that so labouring ye ought to support the weak, and to remember the words of the Lord Jesus, how he said, It is more blessed to give than to receive."*

However, it will only be a blessing if you understand how to give. 2 Corinthians 9:6-8 state *"But this I say, He which soweth sparingly shall reap also sparingly; and he which soweth bountifully shall reap also bountifully. Every man according as he purposeth in his heart, so let him give; not grudgingly, or of necessity: for God loveth a cheerful giver. And God is able to make all grace abound toward you; that ye, always having all sufficiency in all things, may abound to every good work"*. This scripture summarizes how we should give. First, we are to give bountifully. In other words, we need to not hold back, but rather to give what is right. Proverbs 23:6-7 (NIV) state *"Do not eat the food of a stingy man, do not crave his delicacies; for he is the kind of man who is always thinking about the cost."* If we are thinking about the cost, we are not giving bountifully. We are being stingy. The scripture also tells us to give cheerfully. If we are concerned about what we "lost" when we give, we are not giving cheerfully.

There is also guidance in this scripture on how much to give. It tells you to give "as you purpose in your heart". In other words, we are to ask God what it is He would have us give, and give as He directs in our heart. Our heart is our innermost being, our spirit man. God speaks Spirit to spirit in our innermost being. As I began to understand giving, it became rather easy for me to give, so easy that I had to learn this scripture from another angle. I had to learn to "not give" when the Lord told me to "not give". I've heard some preachers state that you should give in every offering. I disagree. This is not backed up in scripture. We need to learn to be obedient to the Spirit in both giving and in not giving.

An additional instruction on how to give is in Malachi 1:13-14 *"Ye said also, Behold, what a weariness is it! and ye have snuffed at it, saith the LORD of hosts; and ye brought that which was torn, and the lame, and the sick; thus ye brought an offering: should I accept this of your hand? saith the LORD. But cursed be the deceiver, which hath in his flock a male, and voweth, and sacrificeth unto the Lord a corrupt thing: for I am a great King, saith the LORD of hosts, and my name is dreadful among the heathen."* When we give, we are to give our best. We are not to give something "second rate". God is a great king and He is worthy of our best.

When we give, it is important to know what to expect when we give, and when to expect it. A number of years ago, a preacher visited my church and spoke a message on giving and receiving. To be honest, looking at it today, I don't believe the message had proper balance, although I believe the heart of the preacher was right with God toward this message, and he gave it with correct motives. In any case, God used him to challenge me on my giving. For over ten years, I had been giving in excess of fifteen percent of my gross income in tithes and offerings. On occasion I had said to God that someday I wanted to be able to give twenty percent. As this preacher spoke, one of the things he did was challenge the congregation to double tithe. In other words, he challenged them to give twenty percent.

The Spirit of God witnessed in me that this was the time for me to step out and give twenty percent. Even though I was giving a lot, this increase was a challenge to me. However, I stepped out and obeyed God. As I increased my giving, I expected to reap a harvest from this giving. Over a year passed and I did not see a harvest. Even my annual merit raise was average at best. I found myself a bit frustrated. One day, as I was reading a book, there was a short section in the book on stewardship and I was convicted about my attitude. I had the wrong attitude in this giving. My attitude was one of "giving to get". I had never done this before. My focus was off. I started giving at this level because God directed me to. However, after a short time, I started looking at the receiving. I was wrong. I repented. Money was not going to be that important to me. I decided that it didn't matter if I reaped from this. It was more important for me to obey God, which is where I started, (but somehow I had gotten off track).

I've heard a number of preachers say that "you can't out-give God". Obviously, He gave His all on the cross and we can never match that. However, the reference of these preachers has always been to money or things money can't buy, not directly to the cross. About two years had passed from when I started giving twenty percent when I saw a harvest. Over a course of less than one year I received salary increases through promotions and merit raises that totaled twenty percent of my salary. I also received bonuses that equaled twenty percent of my salary. In one year God made up for everything I gave in both tithes and offerings for two years!

So what do we really need to expect when we give? First, we should expect that all of our needs will be met. *"But my God shall supply all your need according to his riches in glory by Christ Jesus."* (Philippians 4:19) Secondly, we should expect that we will receive more than we gave. *"Give, and it shall be given unto you; good measure, pressed down, and shaken together, and running over, shall men give into your bosom. For with the same measure that ye mete withal it shall be measured to you again"* (Luke 6:38)

When can we expect to receive? The Bible tells us we will reap "in due season". We will receive when we need it. *"Be not deceived; God is not mocked: for whatsoever a man soweth, that shall he also reap. For he that soweth to his flesh shall of the flesh reap corruption; but he that soweth to the Spirit shall of the Spirit reap life everlasting. And let us not be weary in well doing: for in due season we shall reap, if we faint not"* (Galatians 6:7-9). God will *"Give us this day our daily bread"* (Matthew 6:11).

God always amazes me when He gives. Ephesians 3:20 states *"Now unto him that is able to do exceeding abundantly above all that we ask or think, according to the power that worketh in us."* After my first daughter was born, both of our cars got rather old and needed to be replaced. Buying two new cars was well beyond us financially. Angel's car was in really bad shape. We also needed a larger vehicle than either one of us had.

We looked at choices and decided we needed both a truck and a car. We decided on a Nissan Pathfinder, which could serve both purposes. We prayed about it, and bought when we felt the release in our Spirit to do so. When we did, we traded in both cars and went with one vehicle.

We stayed with only one car for about two years. I can tell you, in today's society, having a single car can be quite a challenge. I really wanted a pickup truck, so I prayed about it, but it was beyond our means. Eventually, Angel got pregnant with our son Andrew and we knew we were going to need another car. I already knew what I wanted. I had been praying about it off and on for about two years. I wanted a Chevrolet C1500 extended cab full size pickup truck. I had done my research and knew just what color I wanted, and what options I wanted. I had even visited a Chevy dealer six months earlier and talked to a Christian salesman named Ken and told him I'd be back to see him when it was time to buy. I had made my list and had prayed over it. I waited for a new truck for a long time. At one point I told the Lord something to the effect of "Lord, I've been waiting for this new truck a long time. When it's time to buy it, I want to be able to drive it off the lot right when I buy it, and not have to wait for prep." One thing that I wanted, but had taken off the list at least six months earlier, when I saw the price of the option, was a power driver's seat.

The time came when we knew it was time to buy the truck. I went to the Chevy dealer on Saturday. The salesman I wanted to see, Ken, was not there. Apparently, he had a death in the family and was at the funeral. I did not want to work with anyone else. I decided to leave my contact information and the list of what I wanted in a truck on Ken's desk.

On Monday, Ken called me to go over my wish list. He said to me, "Joe, what you want is a pretty straightforward truck. However, can you pick a different color. There is not a black one in a five state area." I was disappointed. I wanted a black truck. However, I gave him my second choice color and told him I'd come to see him that evening after work. As I drove across town as part of my job that afternoon, I told the Lord I was disappointed. I had already given up on my power driver's seat since it cost too much, and now it looked like I wasn't even going to get the color of truck I wanted.

That evening when I arrived at the Chevy dealer, Ken told me that my second choice color was not available either. Noting my disappointment he said, "We're the largest Chevrolet truck dealer in the Dallas-Fort Worth area, we have lots of trucks on the lot. Let's drive the golf cart around the lot and see if there is something you're interested in." We drove the lot. They had many trucks, but we didn't see anything I wanted. Most of them were pretty heavily customized and I was looking for a more basic truck.

Ken didn't give up. He said "This is not all the trucks we have. We usually have some out in the service area." So we drove over and looked in the service area. There were a few trucks there, but nothing like what I wanted. As we drove the golf cart up across the front of the dealership on the way back to Ken's office, Angel spotted a black, extended-cab pickup truck up front and said "What about that truck?"

Ken stopped the golf cart and said "Oh, that's a demo." I got out and looked at it. It had the colors I wanted inside and out. It had the 350 V8 engine I wanted. It had the right transmission. It had the right alloy wheels. It had the chrome tie rails that I wanted to have added already on it, and a bed liner I wanted already installed. It also had a power driver's seat! The mileage on it was about 5000 miles. It also had a couple of other really nice options, that weren't on my wish list, already installed. The only thing it didn't have from my list was the tinted windows I wanted, but these would have to be added on any truck.

I said to Ken, "I'm not opposed to buying a demo, but I get a really good deal through this fleet buying service and only pay $500 above invoice for a brand new vehicle. That is usually the same price you sell demos for."

Ken answered, "You're right, but I can sell you this one at cost. I'll get the invoice to prove it."

I looked at the truck. It was everything I wanted, including the power driver's seat! The few added options above my list were nice features that really added to the truck value. The price was a bit higher than I planned, but I had peace about the truck

I told Ken, "I'll take it." We took care of the paperwork and I said to him, "When can I pick it up?"

Ken tossed me the keys and said "Take it with you tonight. Bring it back empty in a week and we'll prep it for you, fill the tank with gas, and put the window tint on. We'll even give you a loaner truck for the day." When he said this, I remembered my prayer to God, asking to be able to drive it home right away without waiting. God gave me everything I wanted, even the power seat I didn't ask for because I thought it was too much money. He did exceedingly more that I asked, and I got to drive it home that night! He did more than I could think! Even though I had asked for that to happen, I never really thought it would. I have never, before or since, bought a new car or truck that I could drive home right after making the deal. God is awesome!

I've shared this already, but probably the most important thing about giving is our attitude in giving.

"If any man teach otherwise, and consent not to wholesome words, even

the words of our Lord Jesus Christ, and to the doctrine which is according to godliness; He is proud, knowing nothing, but doting about questions and strifes of words, whereof cometh envy, strife, railings, evil surmisings, Perverse disputings of men of corrupt minds, and destitute of the truth, supposing that gain is godliness: from such withdraw thyself. But godliness with contentment is great gain. For we brought nothing into this world, and it is certain we can carry nothing out. And having food and raiment let us be therewith content. But they that will be rich fall into temptation and a snare, and into many foolish and hurtful lusts, which drown men in destruction and perdition. For the love of money is the root of all evil: which while some coveted after, they have erred from the faith, and pierced themselves through with many sorrows. But thou, O man of God, flee these things; and follow after righteousness, godliness, faith, love, patience, meekness." (1 Timothy 6:3 - 11)

This message is clear. Do not think that godliness or giving is a means to gain. We should expect to receive, but be careful not to "give to get". We have to be sure we stay away from the love of money. We need to be content in our giving and in our receiving, and sometimes in the lack of receiving, and remember that *"God is faithful"* (1 Corinthians 1:9). Our job is to *"seek ye first the kingdom of God, and his righteousness; and all these things shall be added unto you"* (Matthew 6:33). God's kingdom is our promised land. If we will do these things, we will never have to worry about money again.

Questions for consideration or discussion

1. Do you worry about money or having enough? Why?

2. Do you think that it is spiritual to be poor? Why or why not?

3. Do you have a personal testimony of God's provision in your life? Describe.

4. Do you tithe - consistently? Why or why not?

5. Do you give offerings above the tithe? Are you specifically giving freewill, alms, first fruits and missions' offerings? Why or why not?

6. When you give, how do you determine what amount to give? Explain.

7. When you give, do you give to get? Explain.

8. What do you expect when you give?

9. Do you ask God specifically for your needs and desires? How do you do this?

Chapter 10
The Good Fight
The Lord Our Banner

*"There shall not any man be able to stand before thee
all the days of thy life" (Joshua 1:5)*

As I write this chapter, our military is fighting a
war in Iraq. Our nation is at war with terrorism and
with the regime of Saddam Hussein who supports
terrorists. Although I once took an oath to support and
defend the constitution of the United States, I am not
one of the ones fighting in this war. Nevertheless, the
outcome is very important to me. The United States
military forces are fighting for me and all the citizens
of the United States. They fight under the banner of the
flag of the United States, where I live and am a citizen.
This flag signifies that the full might and authority of
the United States of America is behind these fighting
forces.

In the same way, the Lord fights my battles
here on earth. The ultimate battle, for my soul, has
already been won on the cross. For Jesus said *"It is
finished"* (John 19:30). Nevertheless, there are still
issues I have to deal with on this earth.   Jesus also
said *"In the world ye shall have tribulation: but be of
good cheer; I have overcome the world"* (John 16:33).
In these issues, the Lord fights our battles. These
battles may come in our jobs, our church or in our
private lives.

After I had started the new job at DSC
Communications that God had miraculously provided
back in 1990, I had many challenges in my new
position. Some of these were just due to being new to
the company. Others were due to the requirements of
my job to change the way things were done. One of the
things that I believed needed to be done was to

136

completely rewrite a document called the Printed Circuit Board Design Rules and Guidelines. It was a major revision that essentially scrapped the current document and started over from scratch.

After I completed the draft copy of this rather long document (about 80 pages), I sent it out for review to key parties. Due to the complexity of the document, I specifically requested that comments be made in a certain way on a certain form. This would allow for a meeting to discuss only the comments and their resolution, rather than require a line-by-line review. Most of the reviewers were very amenable to this proposal.

One man, however, in a key position, decided he didn't like the method. He also didn't like the document. He proceeded to mark up his copy of the draft with red ink. He also wrote a number of rather vicious comments, not about the document, but personal attacks on me, in his review. I had done nothing to warrant this attack. Instead of coming to me with these comments and concerns, he took them to my boss's boss, two levels above me, and complained to him.

My boss's boss came to see me, with significant concern. My natural reaction would have been to counterattack in defense. However, I had learned that this was not God's way. *"Dearly beloved, avenge not yourselves, but rather give place unto wrath: for it is written, Vengeance is mine; I will repay, saith the Lord"* (Romans 12:19). I listened closely and just asked to see the marked up document, promising to address the issues.

A quick reading of the comments and the accusations tempted me to get very angry. However, I held my ground and did not do so. I prayed for God's wisdom and direction on how to handle this situation. I decided to address the technical comments in writing and ignore the personal attacks. This was not a small undertaking. I had to write a 25 to 30 page document addressing each and every issue in a factual manner. I determined not to take issue with any of the personal comments.

After I completed this, I gave a copy to my boss's boss. After he read it, his concerns with me vanished and he went and dealt with this man. After he had done so, I went to him and acting like there were no personal attacks, calmly gave him a copy of the answers to his comments. I knew that I still had a major hurdle ahead, since this man was one of those that would have to sign the document before its final release.

This man was also in a position to make my job very difficult. I needed to make changes in the way the company was doing business. His department was a key area that had to be on board with the changes. Although we worked through the design rules document, he continued to fight every change that affected him or his department, whether or not it made any sense. He was a real obstacle. I prayed about this issue on numerous occasions.

Just when it looked like he was going to become an insurmountable obstacle preventing me from achieving what I needed to do, the company went through a business downturn. He was laid off. I experienced Dueteronomy 28:7 in my life *"The LORD shall cause thine enemies that rise up against thee to be smitten before thy face: they shall come out against thee one way, and flee before thee seven ways."* He was replaced with a man who had previously worked for him that supported me, but would not buck his boss. This man readily implemented the changes and became an ally that worked with me toward common interests for the next ten years. God had fought my battle and given me victory and favor. I did not have to fight personally in this battle.

Challenges similar to this can also happen in the church. Our *"adversary the devil, as a roaring lion, walketh about, seeking whom he may devour"* (1 Peter 5:8), will oppose all those who are determined to serve God. One time, there was an issue involving a woman in my care group (a home fellowship group associated with the church). Jenny (not her real name), a member of this care group, had been having a very difficult time. Here husband had divorced her, her oldest son was using cocaine, and her financial situation was very difficult. She had many problems, not the least of which was serious unforgiveness towards her father. The Lord had used me, along with some other members of our care group, to minister to her.

During a telephone discussion between Jenny and the care group leader, he apparently told her that she was insane and needed to seek psychiatric counseling. Needless to say, this upset her greatly. She called me. I calmed her down and pretty much told her to ignore it. Obviously it was hard for her to do. After she hung up, I called the care group leader and confronted him on this. I agreed with him that Jenny had problems, but she was not insane. Calling her insane was not going to help. What Jenny needed was people to care and genuinely love her as a person.

This care leader took a major issue with me confronting him. He accused me of being rebellious and insisted that I had no right to disagree with him on this. He decided to raise this up in the church authority and make an issue of it. He set up a meeting with the touch pastor and one of the elders (a full time staff pastor) to "deal with me" on this. I had not been rebellious and I knew that I was to stand my ground. I had peace about this meeting, although I was essentially "on trial".

Prior to the meeting, the Lord gave me the following scriptures. *"And when the servant of the man of God was risen early, and gone forth, behold, an host compassed the city both with horses and chariots. And his servant said unto him, Alas, my master! how shall we do? And he answered, Fear not: for they that be with us are more than they that be with them"* (2 Kings 6:15-16). I knew that it would be okay. God would fight this battle for me. The meeting was held and I stood my ground. The pastor ended up dealing with this issue with wisdom. I came out of it essentially "acquitted". The care leader even ended up agreeing that calling Jenny insane was not a good thing. Somehow, even my relationship with the care leader ended up okay. The Lord took care of this as He had promised to do.

The Bible repeatedly gives us the principle to depend upon God when we are wrongfully attacked. The story of Jehoshaphat, King of Judah, when he was threatened by the combined armies of the Ammonites, Moabites and Edomites is an excellent example:

> *It came to pass after this also, that the children of Moab, and the children of Ammon, and with them other beside the Ammonites, came against Jehoshaphat to battle. Then there came some that told Jehoshaphat, saying, There cometh a great multitude against thee from beyond the sea on this side Syria; and, behold, they be in Hazazontamar, which is Engedi. And Jehoshaphat feared, and set himself to seek the LORD, and proclaimed a fast throughout all Judah. And Judah gathered themselves together, to ask*

140

help of the LORD: even out of all the cities of Judah they came to seek the LORD. And Jehoshaphat stood in the congregation of Judah and Jerusalem, in the house of the LORD, before the new court, And said, O LORD God of our fathers, art not thou God in heaven? and rulest not thou over all the kingdoms of the heathen? and in thine hand is there not power and might, so that none is able to withstand thee? Art not thou our God, who didst drive out the inhabitants of this land before thy people Israel, and gavest it to the seed of Abraham thy friend for ever? And they dwelt therein, and have built thee a sanctuary therein for thy name, saying, If, when evil cometh upon us, as the sword, judgment, or pestilence, or famine, we stand before this house, and in thy presence, (for thy name is in this house,) and cry unto thee in our affliction, then thou wilt hear and help. And now, behold, the children of Ammon and Moab and mount Seir, whom thou wouldest not let Israel invade, when they came out of the land of Egypt, but they turned from them, and destroyed them not; Behold, I say, how they reward us, to come to cast us out of thy possession, which thou hast given us to inherit. O our God, wilt thou not judge them? for we have no might against this great company that cometh against us; neither know we what to do: but our eyes are upon thee. And all Judah stood before the LORD, with their little ones, their wives, and their children.

Then upon Jahaziel the son of Zechariah, the son of Benaiah, the son of Jeiel, the son of Mattaniah, a Levite of the sons of Asaph, came the Spirit of the LORD in the midst of the congregation; And he said, Hearken ye, all Judah, and ye inhabitants of Jerusalem, and thou king Jehoshaphat, Thus saith the LORD unto you, Be not afraid nor dismayed by reason of this great multitude; for the battle is not yours, but God's. Tomorrow go ye down against them: behold, they come up by the cliff of Ziz; and ye shall find them at the end of the brook, before the wilderness of Jeruel. Ye shall not need to fight in this battle: set yourselves, stand ye still, and see the salvation of the LORD with you, O Judah and Jerusalem: fear not, nor be dismayed; to morrow go out against them: for the LORD will be with you. And Jehoshaphat bowed his head with his face to the ground: and all Judah and the inhabitants of Jerusalem fell before the LORD, worshipping the LORD. And the Levites, of the children of the Kohathites, and of the children of the Korhites, stood up to praise the LORD God of Israel with a loud voice on high.

And they rose early in the morning, and went forth into the wilderness of Tekoa: and as they went forth, Jehoshaphat stood and said, Hear me, O Judah, and ye inhabitants of

142

Jerusalem; Believe in the LORD your God, so shall ye be established; believe his prophets, so shall ye prosper. And when he had consulted with the people, he appointed singers unto the LORD, and that should praise the beauty of holiness, as they went out before the army, and to say, Praise the LORD; for his mercy endureth for ever. And when they began to sing and to praise, the LORD set ambushments against the children of Ammon, Moab, and mount Seir, which were come against Judah; and they were smitten. For the children of Ammon and Moab stood up against the inhabitants of mount Seir, utterly to slay and destroy them: and when they had made an end of the inhabitants of Seir, every one helped to destroy another. And when Judah came toward the watch tower in the wilderness, they looked unto the multitude, and, behold, they were dead bodies fallen to the earth, and none escaped." (2 Chronicles 20:1-24)

Jehoshaphat and the people of Judah humbled themselves, fasted and petitioned the Lord for deliverance. God answered and promised them they would not have to fight this battle. He put the praise singers in front of the army. As they praised the Lord, He set "ambushments" against their enemies. They won the battle without even having to fight. God will do the same for us.

In addition to trusting God there are times we have to fight in the spirit realm under the "banner of the Lord", just as our armed forces fight under the banner of the United States flag. *"For we wrestle not against flesh and blood, but against principalities, against powers, against the rulers of the darkness of this world, against spiritual wickedness in high places."* (Ephesians 6:12) Jehoshaphat fought in the spirit with prayer, fasting, and praise. These are also our weapons. *"For the weapons of our warfare are not carnal, but mighty through God to the pulling down of strong holds; Casting down imaginations, and every high thing that exalteth itself against the knowledge of God, and bringing into captivity every thought to the obedience of Christ"* (2 Corinthians 10:4-5) We also have *"the sword of the Spirit, which is the word of God"* (Ephesians 6:17).

Just as our U.S. armed forces are backed up by the power and authority of the United States of America, we are backed up by the full power and authority of the Lord Jesus Christ. *"And Jesus came and spake unto them, saying, All power is given unto me in heaven and in earth. Go ye therefore, and teach all nations, baptizing them in the name of the Father, and of the Son, and of the Holy Ghost"* (Matthew 28:18-19).

To enter the kingdom of God fully requires effectual spiritual warfare. James 5:16 states *"The effectual fervent prayer of a righteous man availeth much."* Whereas Joshua and the Israelites had to enter their promised land by physical warfare (and yes, there was also a spiritual aspect), we must enter our promised land with spiritual warfare. Jesus said *"the kingdom of heaven suffereth violence, and the violent take it by force"* (Matthew 11:12). He also said *"Think not that I am come to send peace on earth: I came not to send peace, but a sword"* (Matthew 10:34).

I was introduced to spiritual warfare praying for my friend Mary Beth, sometime after I began to pray the Lord's Prayer as an outline. Prior to this time, I had heard about spiritual warfare, but I really did not understand it nor had I truly experienced it. A couple of weeks before this, Mary Beth had received a word from a pastor that satan was going to attempt to drive her insane. At the time, it seemed a rather strange word. One Tuesday evening, I came home from work, and really didn't have anything to do. I picked up the phone and called Mary Beth, but did not get an answer. I had noticed her car was home when I came in (her apartment was right near mine), so I decided I'd go knock on her door to make sure she was okay. She had skipped church on Sunday and I was a bit concerned. (If memory serves correct, she had also missed a few other services just prior to this.)

When I knocked on the door, Mary Beth was home, but was not herself. She acknowledged that she was home, but other than to tell me to go away, she would not even talk to me. She would not answer or come to the door. Something was wrong for sure, but I did not have any idea what. I persisted a bit to see if I could help or determine what was wrong, but it was to no avail.

As I finally gave up and left, I was angry. I was not angry at Mary Beth. I was angry at the devil. I had enough of him messing with my friends. I walked into my apartment and began to pray. I did not pray quietly. I prayed loud. I prayed hard. I warred against the devil in my prayers. I spoke to him with anger and commanded him to let go of my friend. I prayed in the spirit and I prayed with my understanding (see 1 Corinthians 14:15). I was not on my knees praying. I was walking and warring "physically" as I prayed. I worked up a sweat praying because I prayed so hard. After about one hour, I finally felt release in my spirit and stopped praying.

The next night, I went to the church's Wednesday night service. Mary Beth was there and I sat down next to her. She was cordial, but still was really not her usual self. The message by the pastor that night was on spiritual warfare. I could really relate to his message! Towards the end of the service, the pastor gave an altar call for people who felt like they were going insane. Mary Beth (and surprisingly about 20 other people) answered this altar call.

As she went forward, I began to pray in the spirit for her. I asked the Lord (praying in tongues and thinking the requests) to touch her "big time". I asked Him to "knock her down" by the power of His spirit so that she would know for sure that He had dealt with the issues. The pastor went forward and individually laid hands on and prayed for each person who had come forward.

As I was praying I could no longer see Mary Beth. I just assumed that she was out of my view behind the others at the front. However, as all were prayed for and they returned to their seats, I saw Mary Beth sprawled out on the floor under the power of the Holy Spirit. She did not return to her seat for at least another five minutes. Apparently, when the pastor touched her to pray for her, she was overcome by the power of the Spirit and ended up on the floor, exactly as I had asked the Lord to do.

From that day on, I saw a change in Mary Beth. Many of the issues in her life changed significantly. She never again went back to the things of the world that she had come out from. Where she had occasionally hung around with the wrong crowd and had messed with drugs, this ended. I never saw her do that again. She broke all her ties with that old crowd. Some time later I introduced her to a friend of mine that she eventually married. She is a godly woman who is raising five children that are all serving the Lord. I did some intercession, but God fought the battle and won the war!

Since that time, I have learned much about spiritual warfare. To be effectual in our warfare we need to understand three things. First we need to understand against whom we fight. Second, we need to know where and how do we get to the place where we fight (our battlefield). Finally, we must know how to fight. Ephesians 6:12 gives us many of these answers. *"For we wrestle not against flesh and blood, but against principalities, against powers, against the rulers of the darkness of this world, against spiritual wickedness in high places."* Our fight is not against the flesh, but against principalities, powers, rulers of the darkness of this world, and spiritual wickedness in high places. We have identified the enemy and we know his location is in the heavenly realms.

To take on and defeat the enemy, we need to take the high ground. When I was a midshipman in the U.S. Navy, I trained with the U.S. Marines. At one point, we trained on how to assault a hill where there was an enemy stronghold. The high ground is strategic in military warfare. It is the same way in the spirit realm. First, we must realize that God *"hath raised us up together, and made us sit together in heavenly places in Christ Jesus"* (Ephesians 2:6). We are sitting with Christ Jesus in the heavenly realms. This is a place far above the enemy of our souls. For God has placed Jesus at his own right hand *"when he raised him from the dead, and set him at his own right hand in the heavenly places, far above all principality, and power, and might, and dominion, and every name that is named, not only in this world, but also in that which is to come"* (Ephesians 1:20-21).

The spiritual high ground is where Jesus is, which is the most holy place. We get to where Jesus is by praise and the blood of Jesus. Psalm 100:4 states *"Enter into his gates with thanksgiving, and into his courts with praise"*. Hebrews 10:19 adds to this

"Having therefore, brethren, boldness to enter into the holiest by the blood of Jesus". The book of Judges tells us that Judah shall be first *"And the children of Israel arose, and went up to the house of God, and asked counsel of God, and said, Which of us shall go up first to the battle against the children of Benjamin? And the LORD said, Judah shall go up first."* (Judges 20:18) The name Judah means praise. Praise is the first step in spiritual warfare. It takes us to the high ground where we are seated with Christ. Judah (praise) was also first when the children of Israel set out. *"All that were numbered in the camp of Judah were an hundred thousand and fourscore thousand and six thousand and four hundred, throughout their armies. These shall first set forth."* (Numbers 2:9) As shown previously, Jehoshaphat sent the praise singers into battle first.

The second thing we need to know is our authority. Our authority is in the name of Jesus. Without him, we have no authority. Mark 16:17 states *"In my **name** shall they cast out devils"* (emphasis added). Also Phillipians 2: 9-10 state *"Wherefore God also hath highly exalted him, and given him a name which is above every name: That **at the name of Jesus** every knee should bow, of things in heaven, and things in earth, and things under the earth"* (emphasis added). When we war in the spirit realm, we use the name of Jesus. When we speak to the devil and "spiritual wickedness", we need to speak with authority, using the name of Jesus. I compare this to commanding a dog. The dog listens when we speak with authority, but ignores us otherwise. The same is true when we speak to our enemy in the spirit.

Finally, we need to know how to fight. We are to use *"the sword of the Spirit, which is the word of God"* (Ephesians 6:17). Just as Jesus did in Luke 4:3-13, we are to speak the word of God.

148

*"And the devil said unto him, If thou be the Son of God, command this stone that it be made bread. And Jesus answered him, saying, **It is written**, That man shall not live by bread alone, but by every word of God. And the devil, taking him up into an high mountain, shewed unto him all the kingdoms of the world in a moment of time. And the devil said unto him, All this power will I give thee, and the glory of them: for that is delivered unto me; and to whomsoever I will I give it. If thou therefore wilt worship me, all shall be thine. And Jesus answered and said unto him, Get thee behind me, Satan: for **it is written**, Thou shalt worship the Lord thy God, and him only shalt thou serve. And he brought him to Jerusalem, and set him on a pinnacle of the temple, and said unto him, If thou be the Son of God, cast thyself down from hence: For it is written, He shall give his angels charge over thee, to keep thee: And in their hands they shall bear thee up, lest at any time thou dash thy foot against a stone. And Jesus answering said unto him, **It is said**, Thou shalt not tempt the Lord thy God. And when the devil had ended all the temptation, he departed from him for a season"* (Luke 4:3-13 emphasis added).

Jesus used the written word of God to rebuke the devil. We should do the same.

So how do we know specifically who and what is the enemy? A machine gun fired in many directions will hit lots of things, but it is not very effective unless it is aimed at a target. A trained soldier with a single shot well aimed can be much more effective at defeating the enemy. To be this effective we need to know two things. First, we need to know specifically who or what is the enemy. In other words, we need to know the specific issue and the spirit behind it. Secondly, we need to have wisdom on what is *the* word to speak in the spirit to defeat the enemy, just as Jesus applied specific written words to defeat the devil.

Proverbs 20:18 (NIV) gives us direction. *"If you wage war, obtain guidance."* John 16:13 tells us specifically where to get this guidance; *"when he, the Spirit of truth, is come, he will guide you into all truth."* We are to get our guidance from the Holy Spirit. The key to effective spiritual warfare is *listening* and hearing God. We are to *"pray with the spirit, and ... pray with the understanding also"* (1 Corinthians 14:15). When we do this, our warfare is effective for *"whatsoever thou shalt bind on earth shall be bound in heaven: and whatsoever thou shalt loose on earth shall be loosed in heaven"* (Matthew 16:19).

The final step in our warfare is the same as we started. We are to finish with praise. The Lord himself finishes the job. *"And when they began to sing and to praise, the LORD set ambushments against (them)... which were come against Judah"* (2 Chronicles 20:22).

Our fight is a fight of faith. *"Fight the good fight of faith"* (1 Timothy 6:12). It is a good fight because we win! However, we will not win the fight of faith if we choose not to fight it. If we do not fight we forfeit what is rightfully ours to the enemy. Those who want to take the kingdom of God must do it by force.

"And the God of peace shall bruise Satan under your feet shortly." (Romans 16:20)

150

Questions for consideration or discussion
1. Are you letting God "look out for you" or are you "looking out for number one"? Explain.
2. Who defends you when you are wrongly accused? Explain.
3. Do you plan revenge on those who wrong you? Explain.
4. What does spiritual warfare mean to you?
5. Consider the following weapons of our warfare:
    i.   The Blood of Jesus
    ii. Your Testimony of God's work in your life
    iii. Prayer
    iv. Fasting
    v.   Praise
    vi. The Word of God
    vii. The Name of Jesus

Discuss or consider these weapons and how you might use them to wrestle against principalities and powers and spiritual wickedness in the heavenly realms.

Chapter 11
Paths of Righteousness
The Lord our Shepherd

"The steps of a good man are ordered by the LORD:
and he delighteth in his way."
(Psalms 37:23)

How many times in your life have you made decisions only to later regret those decisions? I know that before I learned to pray and walk with God that I sure made my share of bad decisions. For example, I should never have gotten married the first time I did. That decision is one of the biggest decisions in life and I made it wrong. Statistics show that over 50 percent of all marriages end in divorce, so it is obvious that I am not alone in this problem. The other bad decisions in my life were not so life changing. However, in every case, my life would have been better had I made the correct decision.

We can't see our future and are not omniscient. However, we have a God who is and who can direct our paths, if we let him. Proverbs 3:5-6 states *"Trust in the LORD with all thine heart; and lean not unto thine own understanding. In all thy ways acknowledge him, and he shall direct thy paths."* What a better deal this is than just making our own decisions! The Lord can even show us some of the things to come in our future. *"Eye hath not seen, nor ear heard, neither have entered into the heart of man, the things which God hath prepared for them that love him. But God hath revealed them unto us by his Spirit"* (1 Corinthians 2:9-10)

Much of this book has referred to being directed of the Lord in one way or another, learning to "walk in the spirit" and follow God in all things. Walking in the spirit is to *"walk not after the flesh, but*

152

after the Spirit" (Romans 8:1). When we learn to do this consistently, God will direct our paths and we will be able to avoid making poor decisions. As I showed in chapter two, God desires to move us in His directions because He loves us. He can direct our path without our even knowing it. How much better to *"hear a word behind thee, saying, This is the way, walk ye in it, when ye turn to the right hand, and when ye turn to the left"* (Isaiah 30:21).

When my friend Kevin had severe allergy problems, he left the Dallas area to try to get away from the source of the allergy. First, he went to west Texas. Eventually, he took off and headed west to the desert somewhere. He left no forwarding information. I did not know where he went and only had a vague idea as to why. From my perspective, he just disappeared. Nobody knew where he went. His old office just said that he quit and they had no further information.

I was concerned about Kevin, and kept feeling like I should contact him, but really didn't know how. I kept having the thought of going to Longview Texas, where Kevin's aunt and grandmother lived to try to track down Kevin. I began to think that this was God's direction for me to do so. One day, while I was talking to Cindy, a mutual friend of both Kevin and I, I told her what I thought God might be leading me to do. During this phone call, the Holy Spirit confirmed this to me clearly. I was to go to Longview and find out about Kevin from his aunt and grandmother.

There was only one problem with this, and it was a big one. I did not know where they lived in Longview. I did not even know their last names, which were different from Kevin's, since they were related to his mother. I had only been there once with Kevin, and he did the driving. To make things more difficult, when Kevin and I went to Longview, we went at night and did not go on a direct route there. We went to

Kilgore first. I was sure that I did not have any idea how to find this place. Nevertheless, I was convinced that the Holy Spirit was directing me to go. The only thing I was sure of was that if I saw the house, I would recognize it.

When Saturday came, I headed east to Longview, about a two and a half hour drive east. I pulled out the map and decided which exit I would take from the interstate highway. Longview is not a small community. It is a good sized city. I really needed the guidance of the Holy Spirit if I had any hope of finding this house and his aunt and grandmother. I had an idea that I hoped would pan out. When I was out there with Kevin, we had eaten dinner at a Mexican restaurant that I believed was nearby. I figured that I could look up all the Mexican restaurants in the phone book and believed I would recognize the one we had eaten in if I saw it. Then I knew I would be close.

After about an hour and a half of driving all over Longview looking at Mexican restaurants, I realized that this was not going to help. I had visited every one of the Mexican restaurants listed in the phone book and did not recognize any of them, nor the neighborhoods that they were in. I realized I had to depend on the Holy Spirit entirely to guide me. For about another hour I drove around praying in the spirit and trying to get guidance from the Lord. Once again this was fruitless.

I had now spent about five hours traveling to and running around Longview and was no closer to finding my destination than I was when I first arrived in Longview. I finally saw something I recognized. It was Longview High School. When I had gone there with Kevin, he had pointed it out as where he went to High School while we were driving around. The problem was, I remembered it as quite some distance away from his aunt and grandmother's house. I had no idea where to go from there.

I stopped the car and prayed. I said "Lord, I've been running all over Longview for over two and a half hours now and I have no idea where to go. I've tried everything I know to do. I know you sent me out here, but unless you direct me otherwise, I am going to go south on this road until it runs into Interstate 20 and go home. I don't know what else to do."

I pulled out and headed south. I traveled a mile or so south. Suddenly, I just knew to turn right. I turned right and after I went not more than one hundred yards I recognized a bridge over a little creek area. I knew I was close. I continued on. Just around the bend, there was the house! The Lord had directed me there. I had been close numerous other times. That north-south road I was on I had been on many times already that day. I had probably driven by that turn at least five times and not made it. My mind was in the way! When I gave up and decided it was God's direction or nothing, I finally received His guidance.

I pulled into the driveway, got out and rang the doorbell. Kevin's grandmother answered the door. I told her I had come from the Dallas area to find out about Kevin. She did not recognize me, nor did she know the details about Kevin. His aunt would be home from work in about an hour if I cared to wait outside. Fortunately, it was a nice day and they had an outdoor swing. I sat on the swing and waited patiently for his aunt to arrive.

When Kevin's aunt arrived, she recognized me immediately (to my relief). She invited me in and we talked for over an hour. I found out all about Kevin and got an address and phone number for him. He was in Yucca Valley California. His mother had gone there with him. Before I left, I shared a small amount of the story about how the Lord directed me to Longview.

After I returned home I called Kevin. His allergies were doing better. I asked about where he was going to church. He told me he had visited a few churches but that "there weren't any good churches around." He also told me his mother was going to some little country church down the road, but he didn't think much of it. He told me his mother was "more crazy than ever". We had been praying together in agreement for his mother for some time, that God would set her free from some major emotional issues in her life. From my discussions with him, I knew his Christian walk was not where it should be. I began to pray about this more than ever.

A month or so later, I had a business trip to Los Angeles. I knew from discussions with Kevin that he was teaching computer classes at a college in Palm Springs. I had an afternoon free during one of the days of my trip and decided I would drive out to Palm Springs and meet him at the college. Fortunately, I was able to get in touch with him in advance and we were able to set up a brief meeting.

During those days, I was working for Texas Instruments and had to travel to Ridgecrest, California every couple of months. I realized that I could arrange my trip around a weekend, save some money for the company, and visit with Kevin in Yucca Valley for the weekend. This would work pretty well if I flew in and out of the Ontario airport in the Los Angeles area, one of the airports best suited for this trip.

My next trip to Ridgecrest, I arranged to spend the weekend in Yucca Valley and visit with Kevin. I left Ridgecrest and drove south through the desert to meet with him. I had directions to his place, once I actually got into Yucca Valley. The trip from Ridgecrest to Yucca Valley is a couple of hours drive. I had to make it after work in the dark. Mostly the roads are marked reasonably well, but more than once

156

at an intersection I was not always sure of the way. In every case, I had the confirmation in my spirit that I was going the right way.

When I pulled into the Yucca Valley area, I was unable to find the turn off the main road onto the dirt road leading to Kevin's place. I studied the directions and drove up and down the road in the area two or three times with no success. I realized that I needed to call him and get some more details on how to find him. I was in the middle of the desert. There was no place to stop and call from.

I drove down the road towards the town of Yucca Valley and saw a little church on the side of the road called "Country Gospel Church". There were cars there and obviously some activity going on, which I figured was a good sign on a Friday night. As I pulled into the parking lot, I wondered out loud "I wonder if I'll be accepted here." The Holy Spirit spoke to me and said "You will."

I opened the door to the church and walked in. The first person I saw was Kevin's mother! I said "I know you!" She said, "Yes, I'm Lamar." I told her it was good to see her and told her I was coming to visit Kevin and could not identify the turnoff in the desert. I really needed some better directions. She introduced me around and I was definitely welcomed. They were very happy to let me use the phone. I was able to get better directions and find the turn off the main road into the desert.

While I was at the little desert church, I was very blessed to see an answer to my prayers for Kevin's mother. She was definitely in much better shape emotionally and spiritually than I had last seen her. This church was good for her. My heart told me Kevin had badly misjudged this little church. I was in for an interesting weekend. Maybe the details of it will fit in this book later. For now I'll stop here on this testimony of God's guidance and direction in my life.

I'm always amazed at how God directs my path. It really happens every day as long as I walk in the spirit, but sometimes His guidance goes against everything that seems to make sense in the natural. For a period of about two and a half years while I was working for Texas Instruments, I traveled to Colorado Springs every month for business.

On one of these trips, on the day I was to go home, there was a heavy fog in the Colorado Springs area. The airport was not officially closed, but no flights were going in and out due to the fog. I really didn't want to stay another day. I needed to go home. My choices were to either go to the airport and hope for my flight to actually come in and leave, reschedule my flight for the next day, or drive to Denver and try to fly home from there. I felt in my spirit that I should go ahead and take my scheduled Delta flight nonstop from Colorado Springs to Dallas.

As I got to the airport and came up to the rental car counter to turn in my keys for my rental car, I got some strange looks from the attendants. A man at the counter told me I should keep my rental car and drive to Denver to try to get a flight home from there. He was there to rent a car to drive to Denver. He said that there had not been a flight in or out of the airport all day. Just the same I turned in my rental car.

Things did not look good. Most people had already given up on the flight for the day. As I got to the gate where my flight was scheduled to leave, there were only about 20 or 30 passengers waiting for what is usually a pretty full flight for well over a hundred passengers. The Spirit of the Lord spoke to me that this flight would go to Dallas that day. The talk among the waiting passengers was very negative. They expected this flight to be canceled. I was convinced I was going home.

The arriving flight was late, unable to land due to the fog. It looked pretty bad. However, about an hour late, the flight landed safely. It was the first flight to come into the airport all day! All the time I was there, not a single flight took off. The talk remained negative. They cleaned and refueled the plane and we boarded, about an hour and a half behind schedule. We pulled away from the gate and taxied out to the runway.

There we sat. Visibility was not adequate for takeoff. We sat on the runway waiting on the fog for about an hour. Suddenly, it cleared just enough and we were away. I arrived in Dallas about two and a half hours behind schedule, very glad I had followed the Holy Spirit and not the circumstances. Had I chosen to follow the circumstances, I would have still been in Colorado.

God is our father. Just as an earthly father, he cares about what we want and need. He knows the future and can direct our paths if we let him. We shall not want as long as we allow the Lord to be our Shepherd. I have come to know him as Shepherd and can identify with David when he wrote Psalm 23:

> *"The LORD is my shepherd; I shall not want. He maketh me to lie down in green pastures: he leadeth me beside the still waters. He restoreth my soul: he leadeth me in the paths of righteousness for his name's sake. Yea, though I walk through the valley of the shadow of death, I will fear no evil: for thou art with me; thy rod and thy staff they comfort me. Thou preparest a table before me in the presence of mine enemies: thou anointest my head with*

oil; my cup runneth over. Surely goodness and mercy shall follow me all the days of my life: and I will dwell in the house of the LORD for ever."

You can know Him this way also. He will lead you to your promised land.

Questions for consideration or discussion

1. Consider bad decisions that you made in your life? Would your life be different is you had God's direction prior to making these decisions? Even so, can you testify now that God has worked even these bad decisions for good in your life?

2. What does "walking in the spirit" mean to you?

3. Can you give a testimony of God's specific direction in some aspect of your life? Did you know that it was Him giving this direction during the time it occurred, or only afterwards?

4. Do God's leadings in your life always seem to make sense at the time? When you followed this guidance in spite of it not making sense, how has it turned out? When you failed to follow this guidance, what happened?

5. Rate your determination to obey the leading of the Spirit in your life.

Chapter 12
What it Takes to Enter Your Promised Land

"The people that do know their God shall be strong, and do exploits" (Daniel 11:32)

Moses brought the children of Israel out of Egypt with mighty signs and wonders to lead them into the promised land. *"The LORD brought us out of Egypt with a mighty hand: And the LORD shewed signs and wonders, great and sore, upon Egypt, upon Pharaoh, and upon all his household, before our eyes: And he brought us out from thence, that he might bring us in, to give us the land which he sware unto our fathers"* (Dueteronomy 6:21-23). For a New Testament believer, Egypt represents the world and the ways of the world. The promised land represents the kingdom of God and the ways of God. The vast majority of those over twenty years of age that left Egypt never entered their promised land. Instead they died in the desert. God met all of their needs in the desert, but it was not a place of blessing. This is similar to believers who get saved and experience God, but never learn to live in the kingdom of God.

Our choices as believers are one of three. One choice, heaven forbid, is that we can go back to the world (Egypt) and its ways. Another choice is that we can stay in the desert and never enter our promised land, as did many of the Israelites. Finally, we can follow the Lord with all our heart and enter into our promised land.

The first thing that happened when the children of Israel left Egypt and crossed the Red Sea is that they went into the wilderness (desert). *"So Moses brought Israel from the Red sea, and they went out into the wilderness of Shur; and they went three days in the*

161

wilderness, and found no water" (Exodus 15:22). To enter our promised land, we also must go through the wilderness. Even Jesus was not exempt from the wilderness experience. *"And Jesus being full of the Holy Ghost returned from Jordan, and was led by the Spirit into the wilderness"* (Luke 4:1).

Jesus spent forty days in the wilderness. The Israelites went into the desert and spent approximately fourteen months at Sinai before heading for the promised land. *"And it came to pass on the twentieth day of the second month, in the second year, that the cloud was taken up from off the tabernacle of the testimony. And the children of Israel took their journeys out of the wilderness of Sinai"* (Numbers 10:11-12). They spent two months traveling to Sinai *"In the third month, when the children of Israel were gone forth out of the land of Egypt, the same day came they into the wilderness of Sinai"* (Exodus 19:1). The trip from Horeb to Kadesh Barnea, just across the Jordan was an eleven day journey. *"There are eleven days' journey from Horeb* (the mountain of God - see Exodus 3:1-12) *by the way of mount Seir unto Kadeshbarnea"* (Dueteronomy 1:2). So we see that at a minimum, the Israelites had to spend almost three months in the wilderness. Likewise, although we will not likely have to go and live in a desert, we can expect to spend time in the wilderness.

After receiving the law and experiencing God's miracles in the wilderness they were given a command to go to the promised land. *"The LORD our God spake unto us in Horeb, saying, Ye have dwelt long enough in this mount: Turn you, and take your journey, and go to the mount of the Amorites, and unto all the places nigh thereunto, in the plain, in the hills, and in the vale, and in the south, and by the sea side, to the land of the Canaanites, and unto Lebanon, unto the great river, the river Euphrates. Behold, I have set the land before you: go in and possess the land which the LORD sware unto your fathers, Abraham, Isaac, and Jacob, to give unto them and to their seed after them"* (Deuteronomy 1:6-8).

Like the Israelites, God's first command to us is to come out from the world (Egypt). *"Wherefore come out from among them, and be ye separate, saith the Lord, and touch not the unclean thing; and I will receive you, And will be a Father unto you, and ye shall be my sons and daughters, saith the Lord Almighty"* (2 Corinthians 6:17-18). As we do this, we become sons and daughters of God and start our journey into the kingdom of God. His command to us is to *"seek ye **first** the kingdom of God, and his righteousness; and all these things shall be added unto you"* (Matthew 6:33 emphasis added). This is our command to go to the promised land.

The Israelites, however, did not all follow God wholeheartedly. They rebelled against God. *"Notwithstanding ye would not go up, but rebelled against the commandment of the LORD your God: And ye murmured in your tents, and said, Because the LORD hated us, he hath brought us forth out of the land of Egypt, to deliver us into the hand of the Amorites, to destroy us. Whither shall we go up? our brethren have discouraged our heart, saying, The people is greater and taller than we; the cities are great and walled up to heaven; and moreover we have seen the sons of the Anakims there. Then I said unto you, Dread not, neither be afraid of them. The LORD your God which goeth before you, he shall fight for you, according to all that he did for you in Egypt before your eyes; And in the wilderness, where thou hast seen how that the LORD thy God bare thee, as a man doth bear his son, in all the way that ye went, until ye came into this place. Yet in this thing ye did not believe the LORD your God"* (Deuteronomy 1:26-32).

Ten of the twelve men that spied out the land gave a bad report. Only Joshua and Caleb gave a good report. The people chose to believe the bad report and refused to follow God. The result was that all of those over twenty years old when they left Egypt died in the desert, except Joshua and Caleb. *"Say unto them, As truly as I live, saith the LORD, as ye have spoken in mine ears, so will I do to you: Your carcases shall fall in this wilderness; and all that were numbered of you, according to your whole number, from twenty years old and upward, which have murmured against me, Doubtless ye shall not come into the land, concerning which I sware to make you dwell therein, save Caleb the son of Jephunneh, and Joshua the son of Nun. But your little ones, which ye said should be a prey, them will I bring in, and they shall know the land which ye have despised. But as for you, your carcases, they shall fall in this wilderness"* (Numbers 14:28-32). Likewise, we make the choice either to follow God's command to seek first His kingdom, or to never enter the promised land of the kingdom of God.

Forty years later, the children of those that died in the desert entered their promised land. Both generations saw the same miracles, and had the same God, the same promises from God, and the same commands. Why did the second generation believe God and enter the promised land while the first generation did not? The lives of Joshua and Caleb give us insight into this.

Two passages of scripture separate Joshua from the rest of the leadership. Exodus 24:13 states *"And Moses rose up, and his minister Joshua: and Moses went up into the mount of God."* Here we see that Joshua went into the presence of God, just as Moses did. Also, Exodus 33:11 states *"And the LORD spake*

164

unto Moses face to face, as a man speaketh unto his friend. And he turned again into the camp: but his servant Joshua, the son of Nun, a young man, departed not out of the tabernacle." Once again, we see that Joshua spent time in the presence of the Lord, where he had come to know the Lord.

We know less of the personal life of Caleb. However, the Lord speaks favorably of him. Numbers 14:24 states "*But my servant Caleb, because he had another spirit with him, and hath followed me fully, him will I bring into the land whereinto he went; and his seed shall possess it.*" Caleb spoke of himself that he followed the conviction of his heart and wholly followed the Lord. "*Then the children of Judah came unto Joshua in Gilgal: and Caleb the son of Jephunneh the Kenezite said unto him, Thou knowest the thing that the LORD said unto Moses the man of God concerning me and thee in Kadeshbarnea. Forty years old was I when Moses the servant of the LORD sent me from Kadeshbarnea to espy out the land; and I brought him word again as it was in mine heart. Nevertheless my brethren that went up with me made the heart of the people melt: but I wholly followed the LORD my God. And Moses sware on that day, saying, Surely the land whereon thy feet have trodden shall be thine inheritance, and thy children's for ever, because thou hast wholly followed the LORD my God*" (Joshua 14:6-9). The Lord declared that only Caleb and Joshua wholly followed the Lord. "*Save Caleb the son of Jephunneh the Kenezite, and Joshua the son of Nun: for they have wholly followed the LORD*" (Numbers 32:12).

There was one other major difference between the first generation that perished in the wilderness and the second generation that entered the promised land. The first generation had been slaves in Egypt. They often talked of going back to Egypt. "*And they said* one to another, *Let us make a captain, and let us return into Egypt"* (Numbers 14:4). They were not wholly committed to following the Lord. The second generation did not know the slavery of Egypt. Instead, they knew the deliverance and the miracles of God. As such they did not have the same unbelief. Hebrews 3:18-19 confirms it was this unbelief that prevented them from entering the promised land. *"And to whom sware he that they should not enter into his rest, but to them that believed not? So we see that they could not enter in because of unbelief."*

We can consider the second generation as being "not of Egypt", or not of "the world". Jesus spoke of His disciples as he prayed and said *"They are not of the world, even as I am not of the world"* (John 17:16). The second generation, not having the "world" in their system, was able to *know* God and trust Him and believe that He would do that which He said. Even so, we must not be of this world. We must *know* God to be able to trust Him.

The eight chapters previous to this one are devoted to knowing God as who He says that He is and His covenant names. The Israelites had the same opportunities to know God in accordance with His covenant, as it applied to them. There are numerous examples of where He revealed Himself to the children of Israel.

In Exodus 12:13 the blood of the lamb was their righteousness. *"And the blood shall be to you for a token upon the houses where ye are: and when I see the blood, I will pass over you, and the plague shall not be upon you to destroy you, when I smite the land of Egypt."* In Exodus 15:2 He is their salvation. *"The LORD is my strength and song, and he is become my salvation."* In Exodus 20:25, He shows that the altar of sacrifice is not a work of human hands. *"If thou wilt make me an altar of stone, thou shalt not build it of hewn stone: for if thou lift up thy tool upon it, thou hast polluted it."*

In Exodus 23:24, the Lord begins to show Himself to be their sanctification and instructs them not to follow the practices of the other nations. *"Thou shalt not bow down to their gods, nor serve them, nor do after their works: but thou shalt utterly overthrow them, and quite break down their images."* Also Leviticus 18:3 states *"After the doings of the land of Egypt, wherein ye dwelt, shall ye not do: and after the doings of the land of Canaan, whither I bring you, shall ye not do: neither shall ye walk in their ordinances."* In Exodus 31:13, He shows that the work of sanctification is His work and declares His name "Jehovah-m'kaddesh". *"I am the LORD that doth sanctify you."* Similarly in Leviticus 21:8 the Lord states *"Thou shalt sanctify him therefore; for he offereth the bread of thy God: he shall be holy unto thee: for I the LORD, which sanctify you, am holy."* Other passages that show this are Exodus 34:15 and Dueteronomy 12:4.

The peace that the Lord provided to the Israelites was a different type of peace than that which we can know today by His Spirit. First, they were commanded to bring peace offerings, which was for peace with God (which we already have access to through Jesus). The priests blessed the Israelites saying *"The LORD lift up his countenance upon thee, and give thee peace"* (Numbers 6:26). Also, the Lord initially directed their path to avoid war. *"And it came to pass, when Pharaoh had let the people go, that God led them not through the way of the land of the Philistines, although that was near; for God said, Lest peradventure the people repent when they see war, and they return to Egypt"* (Exodus 13:17).

The Lord regularly showed the Israelites of His constant presence. *"And the LORD went before them by day in a pillar of a cloud, to lead them the way; and by night in a pillar of fire, to give them light; to go by day and night: He took not away the pillar of the cloud by day, nor the pillar of fire by night, from before the people"* (Exodus 13:21-22). In Exodus 33:14, the Lord stated *"My presence shall go with thee."* Additionally, the Lord commanded His people not to defile the land for He dwelled among them. *"Defile not therefore the land which ye shall inhabit, wherein I dwell: for I the LORD dwell among the children of Israel"* (Numbers 35:34).

The Lord revealed Himself as their healer also. First, as they departed Egypt, Psalms 105:37 states *"there was not one feeble person among their tribes."* In Exodus 15:26 He revealed His covenant name Jehovah-rophe and stated *"If thou wilt diligently hearken to the voice of the LORD thy God, and wilt do that which is right in his sight, and wilt give ear to his commandments, and keep all his statutes, I will put none of these diseases upon thee, which I have brought upon the Egyptians: for I am the LORD that healeth thee."* At Marah, the Lord healed the bitter waters so the Israelites could drink *"And he cried unto the LORD; and the LORD shewed him a tree, which when he had cast into the waters, the waters were made sweet"* (Exodus 15:25).

Daily, the Lord proved to the Israelites that He was their provider. As they left Egypt, at the word of the Lord, they plundered the Egyptians. *"Speak now in the ears of the people, and let every man borrow of his neighbour, and every woman of her neighbour, jewels of silver, and jewels of gold. And the LORD gave the people favour in the sight of the Egyptians"* (Exodus 11:2-3). Psalms 105:37 confirms that this happened. *"He brought them forth also with silver and gold."* In the wilderness they had no other source but God. One example of this is the daily provision of manna, bread from heaven. *"Then said the LORD unto Moses, Behold, I will rain bread from heaven for you; and the people shall go out and gather a certain rate every day, that I may prove them, whether they will walk in my law, or no"* (Exodus 16:4). He also provided meat to eat and water to drink. *"And it came to pass, that at even the quails came up, and covered the camp"* (Exodus 16:13). *"Behold, I will stand before thee there upon the rock in Horeb; and thou shalt smite the rock, and there shall come water out of it, that the people may drink"* (Exodus 17:6). God miraculously provided that their clothes did not wear out and their shoes continued to fit. *"Thy raiment waxed not old upon thee, neither did thy foot swell, these forty years"* (Deuteronomy 8:4). This was repeated in Deuteronomy 29:5. *"And I have led you forty years in the wilderness: your clothes are not waxen old upon you, and thy shoe is not waxen old upon thy foot."*

God revealed many times that He was their banner and would fight their battles. The first of these was immediately after the Israelites left Egypt and were pursued by Pharoah's army. *"And Moses said unto the people, Fear ye not, stand still, and see the salvation of the LORD, which he will shew to you to day: for the Egyptians whom ye have seen to day, ye shall see them again no more for ever. The LORD shall fight for you, and ye shall hold your peace"* (Exodus 14:13-14). In Exodus 15:3 the people of Israel sang in victory *"The LORD is a man of war: the LORD is his name."* After the defeat of the Amalekites, as Moses hands were lifted up during battle, *"Moses built an altar, and called the name of it Jehovahnissi: For he said, Because the LORD hath sworn that the LORD will have war with Amalek from generation to generation"* (Exodus 17:15-16).

Finally, the Lord daily provided evidence that He was their shepherd, leading and guiding them.

"And the LORD went before them by day in a pillar of a cloud, to lead them the way; and by night in a pillar of fire, to give them light; to go by day and night" (Exodus 13:21). Their every move was directed by the Lord through the cloud and fire. *"And when the cloud was taken up from the tabernacle, then after that the children of Israel journeyed: and in the place where the cloud abode, there the children of Israel pitched their tents. At the commandment of the LORD the children of Israel journeyed, and at the commandment of the LORD they pitched"* (Numbers 9:17-18).

From this we can see that all the Israelites of both generations had the opportunity to get to know God in the wilderness. Of the first generation, only Joshua and Caleb actually entered the promised land. The key differences in these two men are that they followed the Lord wholeheartedly and decided to believe God. Their words were in accordance with their convictions, by faith and not by sight. It is clear that Joshua spent time with God to get to really know Him. These men knew God well enough to trust Him and follow His command, forty years later, to enter their promised land.

Like Joshua, we need to spend time with God. We do this by prayer, praise, and reading the written word of God. If we specifically desire to know God and His ways, and acknowledge His covenant names daily, He will reveal Himself to us. We must speak God's word regardless of the situation. When we do these things, then the Lord will lead us into our promised land, and we will have faith enough, because we know Him, to obey Him. We will know, for sure, that He will do that which He has promised.

Questions for consideration or discussion

1. Consider your life today. Are you

   a. Living like the world and according to the world's system (in Egypt)?

   b. In the wilderness?

   c. In your promised land, the kingdom of God, trusting God for everything and receiving His blessings?

2. Do you know who God is and trust Him sufficiently to follow Him to your promised land? Can you give a testimony of God for each of His covenant names in your life? If not, are you willing and ready to ask God to reveal Himself to you in each of these ways, so that you may know Him and know His ways?

3. Do the words that you speak line up with God's promises and His word, or are they filled with doubt and defeat? Are you ready to ask God to help you rule your tongue so that it lines up with His word?

Chapter 13
Key to the Kingdom

"And I will give unto thee the keys of the kingdom of heaven: and whatsoever thou shalt bind on earth shall be bound in heaven: and whatsoever thou shalt loose on earth shall be loosed in heaven." (Matthew 16:19)

The Lord's Prayer is an outline. As I've previously shared, this was a revelation to me that ultimately changed my life. Based on my experience, very few Christians pray this way. Even some that have had teaching in this area don't pray this way. In many cases, based on my discussions with them, they did it for a while then went back to praying some other way.

The Bible documents two separate and distinct times that Jesus gave teachings on prayer. Both of these, Matthew chapter six, and Luke chapter eleven, are virtually identical. The context of these teachings makes it clear that these were at separate times, probably more than one year apart. When His disciples asked *"Lord, teach us to pray"* (Luke 11:1), His answer was what we call the Lord's Prayer:

> *"Our Father which art in heaven, Hallowed be thy name. Thy kingdom come. Thy will be done in earth, as it is in heaven. Give us this day our daily bread. And forgive us our debts, as we forgive our debtors. And lead us not into temptation, but deliver us from evil: For thine is the kingdom, and the power, and the glory, for ever. Amen"* (Matthew 6:9-13. Luke 11:2-4 says the same thing with the exception that the last statement is absent.)

The fact that Jesus gave us the same answer twice does not surprise me, since the Lord changes not. *"I am the LORD, I change not"* (Malachi 3:6). Since this is the way that Jesus taught us to pray, I would expect to find out that He also prayed the same way. We know from scripture that Jesus spent many hours in prayer, and occasionally even spent the entire night in prayer. *"He went out into a mountain to pray, and continued all night in prayer to God"* (Luke 6:12). We also know that he did not "just" "say the words" of the Lord's Prayer. If you say these at an average pace, they take about 17 seconds to recite. If you say them deliberately, it takes about 25 seconds to say them. This will hardly fill a night in prayer.

We can also be quite sure that He did not endlessly repeat these words. Not only would that be mind numbing, it is completely contrary to His own teaching. *"But when ye pray, use not vain repetitions, as the heathen do: for they think that they shall be heard for their much speaking"* (Matthew 6:7). So we know how He did not pray. The only situation in the Bible that records any significant amount of the prayers of Jesus is the recording of His prayers just prior to His death. A portion of His prayers in the garden of Gethsemane are recorded in three of the four Gospels.

Matthew 26:40 shows us that He prayed for at least an hour. *"And he cometh unto the disciples, and findeth them asleep, and saith unto Peter, What, could ye not watch with me one hour?"* Matthew also records the subject of His prayers. *"And he went a little further, and fell on his face, and prayed, saying, O my Father, if it be possible, let this cup pass from me: nevertheless not as I will, but as thou wilt"* (Matthew 26:39). This is also recorded in Matthew 26:42-44. *"He went away again the second time, and prayed, saying, O my Father, if this cup may not pass away from me, except I drink it, thy will be done. And he came and found them asleep again: for their eyes were heavy. And he left them, and went away again, and prayed the third time, saying the same words."* We clearly see Him praying in accordance with His teaching. He was praying *"thy will be done on earth as it is in heaven"* (Matthew 6:10).

Mark's gospel records this virtually identically. *"And he said, Abba, Father, all things are possible unto thee; take away this cup from me: nevertheless not what I will, but what thou wilt"* (Mark 14:36). Likewise the gospel of Luke records *"Saying, Father, if thou be willing, remove this cup from me: nevertheless not my will, but thine, be done"* (Luke 22:42). In each case we see Him praying in accordance with a portion of His own teaching on prayer. In no case does the Bible attempt to portray this as "all the words" that Jesus spoke in prayer during that hour. On the cross, we even see Jesus pray *"Father, forgive them; for they know not what they do"* (Luke 23:24) in accordance with Matthew 6:12 *"as we forgive our debtors."*

In John's gospel chapter 17, we get an account of a prayer of Jesus in a setting among His disciples. The location for this is apparently the upper room after celebrating the Passover with His disciples prior to going to Gethsemane. Since the length of this prayer is just over two minutes, we would not expect to see all elements of the Lord's Prayer in it. However, even though this short prayer is obviously given not only as a prayer, but also as a teaching to the disciples, it has elements of the Lords prayer in it. In this prayer, we find Jesus looking up to heaven and addressing God as Father. *"These words spake Jesus, and lifted up his eyes to heaven, and said, Father"* (John 17:1). This, of course, lines up with Matthew 6:9 *"Our Father which art in heaven"*. We also find Jesus praying for God to

174

"protect them from the evil one" (John 17:15, NIV) which is in accordance with Matthew 6:13 *"deliver us from evil"*. We also see this prayer petitioning the Father for things that are the will of God for the disciples. *"Thy will be done"* (Matthew 6:10).

In any case, though the vast majority of the prayers of Jesus are not recorded, we can ascertain that they were in accordance with His own teachings on prayer (although I'm quite sure that He never had to pray for His own forgiveness as He was sinless). We can also see from these few recorded prayers that His interpretation of this teaching on prayer is that it is an outline. I've been told, but have not personally confirmed, that it was common for the teachers of that day to teach in outline form. This also backs up this position.

Considering that the apostles followed the teachings of Christ, we would expect that they would also pray the Lord's Prayer. Acts 2:42 states *"And they continued stedfastly in the apostles' doctrine and fellowship, and in breaking of bread, and in prayers."* The actual Greek text here says "in *the* prayers". Although not conclusive, the word "the" refers to specific prayers, which we would expect to be in accordance with the teachings of Jesus on prayer. As with Jesus, there is very little recorded on the actual prayers of the disciples.

Sometimes I have found it difficult to be fervent in prayer. Virtually every time I pray, I *do* experience the manifest presence of God. That is what brings me back to prayer every day. However, at times it seems to me that I'm praying pretty much the same prayers every day, although generally with different words. I seem to be in a rut. Over the years, a couple of times, I have thought about "changing" the way that I pray. Then I think, "How else would I pray?" I sure don't know better than Jesus.

175

Before I learned to pray the Lord's Prayer as an outline, for all practical purposes, I really didn't know how to pray at all. I always come back to the conclusion that His way is the best way. It brings an order, balance, and discipline to my prayer life, which reflects in my entire life. The entire Lord's Prayer is about the kingdom of God. Not one subject in this outline deviates from that purpose. It has been the key to changing my life and living in the kingdom of God. I am convinced that there is no better way to pray.

"Our Father which art in heaven" (Matthew 6:9)

To be like a child and enter the kingdom of God, we must have a Father in the kingdom. As we start to pray, we pray acknowledging Him as our Father. We acknowledge that He loves us as a Father. We receive Him as our Father. We recognize in Him the attributes of the very best Father that we can imagine, better than the best earthly Father. Over a period of time, He will reveal Himself to us so we can know Him as our personal Father in heaven.

"Hallowed be thy name." (Matthew 6:9)

Most of this book has been devoted to the covenant names of God and to getting to know God as whom He says that He is. Psalm 9:10 states *"they that know thy name will put their trust in thee."* As we pray and hallow the name of the Lord, we acknowledge that the blood of Jesus has bought this covenant to us. God inhabits our praises (Psalm 22:3). We take our place in the heavenly realms seated with Christ Jesus (Ephesians 2:6). As we come to know God, we can then trust Him for everything, just like a child trusts his father, and we will come into the kingdom of God. I cannot stress enough how important this part of the

176

Lord's Prayer is. If you don't know you God really is, it will be impossible to truly live in the Kingdom of God on earth as it is in heaven.

"Thy kingdom come. Thy will be done in earth, as it is in heaven." (Matthew 6:10)

After spending time acknowledging the Father and hallowing His name, we come to the part of the prayer that sets our life in order and into the kingdom. With the authority of one seated with Christ in the heavenly realms we "command" that the kingdom of God come and the will of God be done on earth as it is in heaven. Each day, the first thing I pray for here is myself. If I am not in the kingdom and in the will of God, my life will be ineffective, at best. I *need* to be in the kingdom. I am determined to walk in God's will for my life. This puts God first in my life. I am seeking *"first the kingdom of God, and his righteousness"* (Matthew 6:33).

The next thing I pray for each day is my family. I pray for the kingdom of God to come and the will of God to be done in each of their lives. No matter how much or how little time I have, I make time to pray for my immediate family, my wife and children. If time permits, I will often extend this to other relatives.

After this, each day I pray for the kingdom of God and the will of God to be done in my church. I pray for the church as a whole and for the pastor and his wife. If time permits, I will often pray for the other leaders of the church, the elders, and the various ministries of the church and specific church members.

Each day I also make time to pray for the lost to be saved. Jesus came *"to seek and to save that which was lost"* (Luke 19:10). The Lord is *"not willing that any should perish, but that all should come to repentance"* (2 Peter 3:9). I also obey the command of Matthew 9:38 to *"Pray ye therefore the Lord of the harvest, that he will send forth labourers into his harvest."* So we know that this is the will of God that we are praying for.

Most days, following this, I pray for my nation and the leadership of the nation, in particular our president. If time permits, I may extend this into other leaders of the nation, state, county, etc. Paul said in 1 Timothy 2:2 that we are to pray *"For kings, and for all that are in authority; that we may lead a quiet and peaceable life in all godliness and honesty."*

I believe that praying this much of the prayer in a specific order, to start our day, also puts the same priorities into our life. It is following the order of the word Jesus spoke to *"be witnesses unto me both in Jerusalem, and in all Judaea, and in Samaria, and unto the uttermost part of the earth"* (Acts 1:8). Here Jerusalem represents ourselves and our families. Judea represents the church. Samaria the "extended" nation of Israel represents our nation, and the uttermost part of the earth represents the rest of the world.

Beyond this, there are many other areas to pray for. We can pray for missionaries, other countries, other ministries, our friends, our neighborhoods and just about any area that needs prayer. With this list, you can see rather easily that spending lots of time in prayer is easy. This also keeps us looking beyond ourselves, which will help us keep from being selfish.

When you pray for the kingdom of God and the will of God in your life or others, it helps to know what the will of God is. The general rule to use for this is that the will of God is in the word of God. If we can apply the word of God specifically, we can *know* that we are praying the will of God correctly. Certain things are obviously God's will. I pray about my role as a husband, that I would love my wife *"even as Christ also loved the church, and gave himself for it"*

(Ephesians 5:25). I determine to leave all others, cleave only to my wife, and become one with her (see Genesis 2:24). I pray for my children. I pray that I would know how to *"Train up a child in the way he should go"* so that *"when he is old, he will not depart from it"* (Proverbs 22:6). I pray that *"all (my) children shall be taught of the LORD; and great shall be the peace of (my) children"* (Isaiah 54:13). There are also other scriptures that help us to pray for our families.

As we pray for the will of God, in our lives and others, there are many things we can pray. However, there are some that we should not overlook. Here is a short list to help get started. First, we need to pray for wisdom. Proverbs 4:7 states *"Wisdom is the principal thing; therefore get wisdom: and with all thy getting get understanding."* Another thing of importance is the fruit of the Spirit for Jesus said *"Bring forth therefore fruits worthy of repentance"* (Luke 3:8). The *"fruit of the Spirit is love, joy, peace, longsuffering, gentleness, goodness, faith, meekness, temperance: against such there is no law"* (Galatians 5:22-23).

We need to pray for boldness as the disciples prayed *"grant unto thy servants, that with all boldness they may speak thy word"* (Acts 4:29). Obedience is also key. *"We ought to obey God"* (Acts 5:29). We need the anointing (God's divine enabling for a specific purpose) in every part of our lives for Jesus said *"without me ye can do nothing"* (John 15:5).

The gifts of the Holy Spirit are also important to pray for. 1 Corinthians 14:1 says *"desire spiritual gifts"* that are delineated in 1 Corinthians 12:8-10. *"For to one is given by the Spirit the word of wisdom; to another the word of knowledge by the same Spirit; To another faith by the same Spirit; to another the gifts of healing by the same Spirit; To another the working of miracles; to another prophecy; to another discerning of spirits; to another divers kinds of tongues; to another the interpretation of tongues."*

Finally it is important that we pray for our heart (our innermost being) and the heart of those that we are praying for. The Bible says *"Keep thy heart with all diligence; for out of it are the issues of life"* (Proverbs 4:23). Some specific things that I find helpful in my walk with the Lord when I pray for my heart include praying for a pure heart in God's eyes. *"There is a generation that are pure in their own eyes, and yet is not washed from their filthiness"* (Proverbs 30:12). Also praying for a hungry heart helps keep us on fire with God. *"Blessed are they which do hunger and thirst after righteousness: for they shall be filled"* (Matthew 5:6). I also think it is important that we pray for a hearing and discerning heart. John 10:4-5 states *"the sheep follow him: for they know his voice. And a stranger will they not follow, but will flee from him: for they know not the voice of strangers."* We should pray for a happy (merry) heart. *"A merry heart doeth good like a medicine: but a broken spirit drieth the bones"* (Proverbs 17:22). Finally, and possibly most important, we need to pray for a humble heart for *"Pride goeth before destruction, and an haughty spirit before a fall"* (Proverbs 16:18).

There is much more to pray for as we pray for the kingdom of God to come, and the will of God to be done, on earth as it is in heaven. My intent here is not to give a recipe to pray by, but rather to provide some scriptural guidance and things that have helped me in my prayer life. By no means is this a complete listing of things to pray for. Similarly, these are not things that "must" be prayed for every day. This listing is to help give some insight into what it really means to pray for the kingdom of God to come. The intent is to help get you into your promised land.

In all these things it is important that we follow the leading of the Holy Spirit. We should pray in our spirit and with our understanding in these areas. *"For we know not what we should pray for as we ought: but the Spirit itself maketh intercession for us with groanings which cannot be uttered"* (Romans 8:26). *"For if I pray in an unknown tongue, my spirit prayeth, but my understanding is unfruitful. What is it then? I will pray with the spirit, and I will pray with the understanding also"* (1 Corinthians 14:14-15).

Give us this day our daily bread (Matthew 6:11)

If we spend our life worrying about our needs, we will entirely miss the kingdom of God. In the Sermon on the Mount, Jesus said:

> *"Therefore I say unto you, Take no thought for your life, what ye shall eat, or what ye shall drink; nor yet for your body, what ye shall put on. Is not the life more than meat, and the body than raiment? Behold the fowls of the air: for they sow not, neither do they reap, nor gather into barns; yet your heavenly Father feedeth them. Are ye not much better than they? Which of you by taking thought can add one cubit unto his stature? And why take ye thought for raiment? Consider the lilies of the field, how they grow; they toil not, neither do they spin: And yet I say unto you, That even Solomon in all his glory was not arrayed like one of these. Wherefore, if God so clothe the grass of the field, which to day is, and to morrow is cast into the oven, shall he not much more clothe you, O ye of little*

faith? Therefore take no thought, saying, What shall we eat? or, What shall we drink? or, Wherewithal shall we be clothed? (For after all these things do the Gentiles seek:) for your heavenly Father knoweth that ye have need of all these things. But seek ye first the kingdom of God, and his righteousness; and all these things shall be added unto you. Take therefore no thought for the morrow: for the morrow shall take thought for the things of itself. Sufficient unto the day is the evil thereof" (Matthew 6:25-34).

How do we truly keep from worrying? The only way I know is to give our needs and cares and worries to God. James tells us in the word that *"ye have not, because ye ask not"* (James 4:2). He also said that when we ask, we don't receive because we ask with the wrong motives. *"Ye ask, and receive not, because ye ask amiss, that ye may consume it upon your lusts"* (James 4:3). Yet, God desires to give us all things. *"He that spared not his own Son, but delivered him up for us all, how shall he not with him also freely give us all things"* (Romans 8:32)? So obviously there is a balance here. We need to check our motives when we ask. We also need to make sure that we are being obedient in our tithing and giving. When we do this, we can ask with confidence and expect to receive.

Proverbs 27:20 says *"the eyes of man are never satisfied."* No matter what we have, there is always something else we want. One of the things that I have done is make lists. I've shared about this before in previous chapters. There are essentially two kinds of lists I make. The first is a specific list about specific parts of something I already know is a true need or God wants me to have. This includes things like new cars, when I need one, a house, such as when God told me to buy one and also when I had more children than the house could reasonably hold and needed a bigger house, and when I asked the Lord for a wife.

The second kind of list I make is a list of what I want. These are typically not needs. (In some cases they might be future needs.) They often are in pursuit of a specific purpose, or just something I think I'd like to have. I write this list down and submit it to God. I only do this once in a while, and occasionally my wife and I might pray over the list together. One thing I've learned is that God knows better what I want or need than I do. I often find that over time as I pray, I will cross things off the list I made, not because I received them, but because I realized that either I didn't really want them, or they might take up too much of my time, or because there was something that better suited what I was looking for.

The list is not a magic formula. It is a tool to help keep me in prayer and balanced. I am also willing to wait and be sure that not only is what I'm asking for God's will for me to have, but also is it the right time for me to buy it. Of course, sometimes I don't have to buy things. People just give them to me. One of the best things about these lists is to go look at them about every six months or so, and see how God has provided those things I have asked for. I can then cross them off the list and thank God for his provision.

I have found that churches don't ask God for their needs. Many times, they might tell the congregation that they need some amount of money for something, but they don't bother to ask God. One of the most powerful things is the prayer of agreement. What could be better than having a church, in a prayer meeting, spend a few minutes praying over the needs of the church and the ministries of the church. If the budget for the church is $5,000 a week, why not ask

God for that specific amount? If the church wants to support another missionary, and needs $500 a week to do so, then why not ask corporately for that increase? Asking the congregation is fine, but the source is God, not the people.

So daily, when you pray for your daily bread, a good guideline is to ask first for the needs of the church as a whole. Next, ask God to provide for those in the church that are financially struggling. After this is done, then ask for the needs that you have for that very day. Occasionally, you can then pray for future needs and wants. This keeps our focus on the kingdom and not on stuff. However, we must understand that God *does* want us to ask Him for our needs and wants.

"And forgive us our debts, as we forgive our debtors"
(Matthew 6:12)

There is not one of us without sin. 1 John 1:8-9 says *"If we say that we have no sin, we deceive ourselves, and the truth is not in us. If we confess our sins, he is faithful and just to forgive us our sins, and to cleanse us from all unrighteousness."* We may walk free from sin (at least that we are aware of) for a few days at a time, but we always need forgiveness. We can ask God to forgive us for the sins we know nothing about. When we are aware of sin in our lives, we also need to ask the Holy Spirit to help us to not do that again.

It is not only ourselves that need God's forgiveness daily. Our family, our church, and our nation need forgiveness. I'm a believer in getting myself right with God first, but the scripture says to pray "forgive us" not just "forgive me." Our church congregations and leaders are in need of forgiveness today, not only for sins of commission, but for sins of omission, where we have failed to do that which God has commanded.

Our nation is in desperate need of forgiveness. This nation was founded to be a Christian nation, yet we have allowed our government to secularize our nation. Many of the practices accepted in our nation today are abhorrent to God. The church must intercede for the nation. 2 Chronicles 7:14 says *"If my people, which are called by my name, shall humble themselves, and pray, and seek my face, and turn from their wicked ways; then will I hear from heaven, and will forgive their sin, and will heal their land."* The condition of the nation is the responsibility of the church.

Jesus also put a high priority on us forgiving others. Immediately after his teaching on prayer, He reinforced this point. *"For if ye forgive men their trespasses, your heavenly Father will also forgive you: But if ye forgive not men their trespasses, neither will your Father forgive your trespasses"* (Matthew 6:14-15). When we are offended, we should be quick to forgive. Ephesians 4:26 says to *"let not the sun go down upon your wrath."* When we come to prayer, we need to ask the Lord to show us any unforgiveness from each day, and decide to forgive right then and there. This is the prescription to prevent a *"root of bitterness"* (Hebrews 12:15) from springing up in our lives.

"And lead us not into temptation, but deliver us from evil" (Matthew 6:13)

Ephesians 4:27 says to *"give (no) place to the devil."* We must *"Be sober, be vigilant; because your adversary the devil, as a roaring lion, walketh about, seeking whom he may devour"* (1 Peter 5:8). We are to *"Submit yourselves therefore to God. Resist the devil, and he will flee"* (James 4:7) from us. We do this first by praying and recognizing our adversary.

We also must *"Put on the whole armour of God, that ye may be able to stand against the wiles of the devil"* (Ephesians 6:11). In the mid 1970's, I was in the Philippines as a Midshipman in the U.S. Navy. During this time, the Philippines were under martial law. The area around the Navy base at Subic Bay was a rough area. When we left the base to go into the town, we put on "our armor". The armor we put on was not physical, nor was it the armor of God. We walked out as a member of the United States Navy. We had the haircuts and we had the walk of military men. We knew, and so did every Philippine native that saw us, that we had the backing of the United States behind us. It helped keep us from trouble.

In the same way, as we prepare to leave our place of prayer where we are intimate with God and go into the world, we need on our spiritual armor. We don't need this in the throne room of God, but we sure need it in the world.

> *"Stand therefore, having your loins girt about with truth, and having on the breastplate of righteousness; And your feet shod with the preparation of the gospel of peace; Above all, taking the shield of faith, wherewith ye shall be able to quench all the fiery darts of the wicked. And take the helmet of salvation, and the sword of the Spirit, which is the word of God: Praying always with all prayer and supplication in the Spirit, and watching thereunto with all perseverance and supplication for all saints"* (Ephesians 6:14-18).

As we prepare to go into the world, we put on the armor by our words and a conscious decision in our hearts to "put on" the armor.

We have the "belt of truth". We establish that the word of God is our truth. We will not be moved from that which we know to be true. The "breastplate of righteousness" covers our hearts. We determine that we are going to live and walk in the righteousness of God today. Our feet are ready to carry us to proclaim the gospel. *"How beautiful upon the mountains are the feet of him that bringeth good tidings, that publisheth peace; that bringeth good tidings of good, that publisheth salvation"* (Isaiah 52:7). We take the "shield of faith". We have faith in God, faith in God's word. We make a decision that we are going to believe and not doubt. We put on the helmet of salvation. We declare that *"we have the mind of Christ"* (1 Corinthians 2:16). We set our mind *"on things above, not on things on the earth"* (Colossians 3:2).

We will take up the *"sword of the Spirit, which is the word of God"* by declaring we will speak the word of God today. We will not speak contrary to the word of God. We will not let any *"corrupt communication proceed out of (our) mouth"* (Ephesians 4:29). We will speak God's word today. Finally, we determine that we will *"pray without ceasing"* (1 Thessalonians 5:17), praying in the Spirit and with our understanding.

In Job 1:10, satan said to God of Job *"Hast not thou made an hedge about him, and about his house, and about all that he hath on every side? thou hast blessed the work of his hands, and his substance is increased in the land."* This is a hedge of protection that we also can have around our lives, our families, our work and our substance.

Psalm 91 tells us how we can receive this. Verse 1 starts off *"He that dwelleth in the secret place of the most High shall abide under the shadow of the Almighty.*" Verse 2 then says "***I will say** of the LORD, He is my refuge and my fortress: my God; in him will I trust*" (emphasis added). These are the words we are to say and believe.

The Lord says that He will protect us and deliver us "*Because thou hast made the LORD, which is my refuge, even the most High, thy habitation*" (Psalm 91:9) and "*Because he hath set his love upon me, therefore will I deliver him: I will set him on high, because he hath known my name*" (Psalm 91:14). The rest of Psalm 91 declares how the Lord will protect and deliver you. If you are praying daily, you are making the Lord your habitation. You have set your love upon the Lord. You will know His name. He will be your God, your refuge, and your fortress in whom you can trust.

For thine is the kingdom, and the power, and the glory, for ever. Amen. (Matthew 6:13)

As the last part of the prayer, we acknowledge and praise Him and thank Him who has made all things possible and who will answer our prayers. The kingdom that we walk in is His kingdom. We did not achieve these things on our own. The power we experience, both to walk in the spirit and to be witnesses with signs and wonders following is His power. We must also determine to remember it is His glory, not ours. "*I am the LORD: that is my name: and my glory will I not give to another*" (Isaiah 42:8). We are not to touch God's glory. As we finish our prayer time in praise, we "*shall go out with joy, and be led forth with peace*" (Isaiah 55:12). The kingdom of God has been established for our day through our prayers. We now get to live in it.

The Lord's Prayer is our key to the kingdom. It opens the promised land to us. There is no doubt that reading the Bible, attending church and the fellowship of the believers are important also. These are also the will of God. However, as good as these are, God holds the intimacy and fellowship of prayer at a higher level. It is also the only thing that will establish us in the kingdom of God on earth as it is in heaven.

Watch ye therefore, and pray always, that ye may be accounted worthy to escape all these things that shall come to pass, and to stand before the Son of man"
(Luke 21:36).

Questions for consideration or discussion
1. Do you pray the Lord's Prayer as an outline? Why or why not?
2. Consider the Lord's Prayer. Does it cover every need in your life? Think about your needs and how they are covered.
3. Are you willing to change the way that you pray to line up with the outline of the Lord's Prayer? Will you continue this for the long run? If so, will you make a commitment to God right now to do so?

Chapter 14
Never Forget

"The blessing of the LORD, it maketh rich, and he addeth no sorrow with it" (Proverbs 10:22)

It is hard to convey how good the reality of living in the kingdom of God is. It is a place that is far better than I know how to describe. This does not mean that there are not trials in my life or that everything is always perfect. However, in all these things there is an inner joy and peace and a knowing that no matter what, things are working for my good. The scripture *"And we know that all things work together for good to them that love God, to them who are the called according to his purpose"* (Romans 8:28) takes on a reality beyond just the words.

The kingdom of God also comes in our lives and gives us our reason for living. As we learn to live in God's kingdom, He clearly reveals to us His specific purpose for our lives. Each of us has a calling in God's kingdom. Ephesians 1:11 says *"In whom also we have obtained an inheritance, being predestinated according to the purpose of him who worketh all things after the counsel of his own will."* It is the purpose of God that fills our lives.

This does not mean that we will all be called into the full time fivefold ministry of the Gospel. It also does not mean that we will be called to be a missionary somewhere we don't want to go. It does mean that we will be witnesses and have a purpose in serving God. However, each specific calling will be in accordance with the desires of our heart. For God gives us *"the desires of (our) heart"* (Psalm 37:4). He puts His desires into our heart and they become our desires.

The kingdom of God is also a place of blessing. This blessing includes but is not limited to financial blessing. My biggest concern here is that I don't convey the kingdom of God as a place of financial blessing without moderating that message. If we get focused on money, we will miss the true riches God has for us. Jesus said in Luke 16:11 *"If therefore ye have not been faithful in the unrighteous mammon, who will commit to your trust the true riches?"* He clearly separates money from true riches.

What really are true riches? They are things that are far better than money. Fellowship with God is an example of true riches. To walk and talk with Jesus is far better than all the wealth of the world! To experience His presence and His glory far surpasses anything that money can buy! A godly and virtuous wife and a loving family also far surpass that which money can buy. To have a home and not just a house is better than all the house that money can buy without it being a true home. To fulfill God's purpose for our life day to day is of much greater value than money. This list could go on, but this sufficiently makes the point.

In any case, as you finish your wilderness experience and begin to live in your promised land, the day will come when God will begin to bless you and it *will* include financial blessing. The message to you will be Haggai 2:19 *"from this day will I bless you"* and you will see a difference in your life. You may not become rich in the sense that the world calls rich, but you will have more than enough. Your needs will be met and then some. In this time it is important that *"thou shalt remember the LORD thy God: for it is he that giveth thee power to get wealth, that he may establish his covenant which he sware unto thy fathers, as it is this day"* (Deuteronomy 8:18). Psalm 62:10 gives us this warning *"if riches increase, set not your heart upon them."*

If we learn to live in this balance and *continue* to seek first God's kingdom, then we will see that *"the wealth of the sinner is laid up for the just"* (Proverbs 13:22). Psalm 112 verses 1 through 3 state *"Praise ye the LORD. Blessed is the man that feareth the LORD, that delighteth greatly in his commandments. His seed shall be mighty upon earth: the generation of the upright shall be blessed. Wealth and riches shall be in his house: and his righteousness endureth for ever."* This is a promise that I have yet to meet a person that didn't want to claim it. Such is the promise of the kingdom of God.

God's word gives us significant warnings related to His blessing us in our promised land:

> *"For the LORD thy God bringeth thee into a good land, a land of brooks of water, of fountains and depths that spring out of valleys and hills; A land of wheat, and barley, and vines, and fig trees, and pomegranates; a land of oil olive, and honey; A land wherein thou shalt eat bread without scarceness, thou shalt not lack any thing in it; a land whose stones are iron, and out of whose hills thou mayest dig brass.*
>
> *When thou hast eaten and art full, then thou shalt bless the LORD thy God for the good land which he hath given thee. Beware that thou forget not the LORD thy God, in not keeping his commandments, and his judgments, and his statutes, which I command thee this day: Lest when thou hast eaten and art full, and hast built goodly houses, and dwelt therein; And when thy herds and thy flocks multiply, and thy silver and thy gold is multiplied, and all that thou hast is multiplied; Then thine heart be lifted up, and thou forget the LORD thy*

God, which brought thee forth out of the land of Egypt, from the house of bondage; Who led thee through that great and terrible wilderness, wherein were fiery serpents, and scorpions, and drought, where there was no water; who brought thee forth water out of the rock of flint; Who fed thee in the wilderness with manna, which thy fathers knew not, that he might humble thee, and that he might prove thee, to do thee good at thy latter end; And thou say in thine heart, My power and the might of mine hand hath gotten me this wealth. But thou shalt remember the LORD thy God: for it is he that giveth thee power to get wealth, that he may establish his covenant which he sware unto thy fathers, as it is this day. And it shall be, if thou do at all forget the LORD thy God, and walk after other gods, and serve them, and worship them, I testify against you this day that ye shall surely perish" (Deuteronomy 8:7-19).

Our promised land is different from that which the Israelites received, but the promises and warnings are much the same. We will not lack for anything but if we forget God and turn away from Him, we will perish and all our wealth will come to nothing.

"Behold, I set before you this day a blessing and a curse; A blessing, if ye obey the commandments of the LORD your God, which I command you this day: And a curse, if ye will not obey the commandments of the LORD your God, but turn aside out of the way

which I command you this day, to go after other gods, which ye have not known" (Deuteronomy 11:26-28).

The "other gods" in this warning, will not likely be images of wood and stone, as they were in the days that this scripture was written. They can be anything that you set your heart upon that might come before God. Things I've seen in this world include the love of money, love of sports, love of hobbies and similar items. All these things can be fine in their proper place, but when they become idols in our lives, we have failed.

"And it shall come to pass, if thou shalt hearken diligently unto the voice of the LORD thy God, to observe and to do all his commandments which I command thee this day, that the LORD thy God will set thee on high above all nations of the earth: And all these blessings shall come on thee, and overtake thee, if thou shalt hearken unto the voice of the LORD thy God. Blessed shalt thou be in the city, and blessed shalt thou be in the field. Blessed shall be the fruit of thy body, and the fruit of thy ground, and the fruit of thy cattle, the increase of thy kine, and the flocks of thy sheep. Blessed shall be thy basket and thy store. Blessed shalt thou be when thou comest in, and blessed shalt thou be when thou goest out. The LORD shall cause thine enemies that rise up against thee to be smitten before thy face: they shall come out against thee one way, and flee before thee seven ways. The LORD shall command the blessing upon thee in thy storehouses,

and in all that thou settest thine hand unto; and he shall bless thee in the land which the LORD thy God giveth thee. The LORD shall establish thee an holy people unto himself, as he hath sworn unto thee, if thou shalt keep the commandments of the LORD thy God, and walk in his ways. And all people of the earth shall see that thou art called by the name of the LORD; and they shall be afraid of thee. And the LORD shall make thee plenteous in goods, in the fruit of thy body, and in the fruit of thy cattle, and in the fruit of thy ground, in the land which the LORD sware unto thy fathers to give thee. The LORD shall open unto thee his good treasure, the heaven to give the rain unto thy land in his season, and to bless all the work of thine hand: and thou shalt lend unto many nations, and thou shalt not borrow. And the LORD shall make thee the head, and not the tail; and thou shalt be above only, and thou shalt not be beneath; if that thou hearken unto the commandments of the LORD thy God, which I command thee this day, to observe and to do them: And thou shalt not go aside from any of the words which I command thee this day, to the right hand, or to the left, to go after other gods to serve them"
(Deuteronomy 28:1-14).

These are the promises of the kingdom of God for obedience. Before I learned to live in the kingdom of God I experienced many of the curses for disobedience, without even knowing that God's word had any. These are listed in Deuteronomy 28 verses 15 through 68. I will not list them here, but as a warning, I recommend that you read them. The laws of God are true whether we know about them or not, just as physical laws such as the law of gravity act upon us whether we know about them or not. Like Isaiah, we must *"set (our) face like a flint,* to serve God*, and (we) know that (we) shall not be ashamed"* (Isaiah 50:7). As we do this, and seek God's kingdom, we will enter our promised land and the promises of the kingdom are ours. These blessings will overtake us (see Deuteronomy 28:2 above).

Our promised land awaits. God has given us the way to go. Prayer, and specifically the Lord's Prayer, will take us there. Start your journey today, and never look back.

"Choose you this day whom ye will serve...but as for me and my house, we will serve the LORD." (Joshua 24:15)

Questions for consideration or discussion

1. Do you know God's specific purpose for you life? What is your "calling"?
2. What are the desires of your heart that God would want to bless you with?
3. What is more important to you, fellowship with God, or His blessings?
4. What is first in your life?
5. If you had to give up everything in your life today, all your possessions, family and friends, could you experience the kingdom of God in your life? Why or why not?
6. Are you ready to make the commitment to serve the Lord all the days of your life, no matter what the cost? If so, make this commitment now.

196

7. Are you ready to take the journey through the wilderness to your promised land? If so, let the Lord know in prayer and get started!